Celtic
Mythology

LIBRARY OF THE WORLD'S
MYTHS AND LEGENDS

Celtic Mythology

Proinsias Mac Cana

NEWNES BOOKS

Celtic Mythology first published 1968.
New revised edition
published 1983 by Newnes Books,
a division of The Hamlyn Publishing Group Limited,
Bridge House, 69 London Road,
Twickenham, Middlesex TW1 3SB, England,
and distributed for them by
Octopus Distribution Services Limited,
Rushden, Northamptonshire, England.

Second Impression 1984
Third Impression 1987

Softback edition first published 1985
For sale in the Republic
of Ireland only.

Hardback ISBN 0 600 34289 1
Softback ISBN 0 600 33281 0

Printed in Yugoslavia

Contents

Introduction

The unity of the Celts of antiquity was one of culture rather than of race. Those peoples whom the Greeks and Romans knew as Celts no doubt were sprung from various ethnic origins, but in the view of external observers they had sufficient shared features – in language and nomenclature, social and political institutions, and in general their way of life – to mark them off as a recognisably distinct nation. So far as the Celts of continental Europe are concerned, we must take the commentaries of Posidonius and his learned progeny largely on trust, since the communities of whom they wrote have long since been merged in other socio-cultural groupings. But the insular Celts remain – albeit in sadly reduced circumstances – and their separate traditions, which are important both in their extent and in their antiquity, not only reveal a close affinity between the cultures of the Irish and the British Celts, but also corroborate some of the more striking factual comments made by classical authors on the Celts of continental Europe.

Moreover, down the ages there is a remarkable consistency in the comments of foreign observers writing about the Celts. Thus, while the popular notion of them as reflected in modern literature has undoubtedly been coloured by eighteenth and nineteenth century romanticism with its susceptibility to mist, magic and melancholy, it certainly did not originate there. In fact, many of the attributes which it ascribes to the Celts – eloquence, lyric genius, volatile temperament, prodigality, reckless bravery, ebullience, contentiousness, and so on – have a much longer lineage, appearing in the accounts by classical authors of two thousand years ago. And

how often, when reading the comments of Elizabethan gentlemen on the native Irish, does one experience the odd sensation of having seen a great deal of it before, in Posidonius and his derivatives to be precise. All of which seems to suggest that ethnological misrepresentations, once they are born, never die – or alternatively, that such abstractions as the 'Celtic character' and the 'Celtic temperament' may ultimately have some basis in reality.

The Rise of the Celts

By the fourth century B.C. the Celts were accounted one of the four peripheral nations of the known world, beside the Scythians, the Indians and the Ethiopians – and not without reason, for already they had begun to intrude themselves, rudely and dramatically, into the affairs of the great Mediterranean centres of political and cultural influence. From their original homeland, which comprised southern Germany and part of Bohemia, they moved with explosive energy to the eastern and western limits of the European continent and threatened the rising power of Rome. By the end of the fifth century the area of Celtic settlement had already been considerably extended beyond its original limits and in Spain Celtic peoples were well established over much of the country following successive immigrations.

Then began a period of further rapid expansion. About 400 B.C. Celtic tribes invaded northern Italy, and while the main body settled there to form what was to be known as Gallia Cisalpina, others advanced on plundering raids throughout the peninsula and in 390 B.C. captured and sacked the city of Rome. To the east, other tribes advanced into the Carpathians and the Balkans where their presence is attested as early as the first half of the fourth century. The general impression is of a continual ferment of movement, whether in search of plunder and mercenary service or merely somewhere to settle. In 279 a section of them entered Greece and plundered the shrine of Delphi, and in the following year three of their tribes, known collectively as Galatae (an equivalent of the commoner term *Keltoi/Celtae*), crossed into Asia Minor and established themselves in the region which still bears the name Galatia.

By this time most of Britain was within the Celtic realm. The earliest immigration which can be confidently defined as Celtic took place in the fifth century B.C., another important influx is dated to the third century, and the final phase was reached with the arrival of the Belgae in the early part of the first century. Ireland presents a still more complicated problem, and widely divergent dates have been proposed for the coming there of the first Celts. As matters stand, however, it is only from about the third century B.C. onwards that the archaeological record permits us to speak with complete assurance of the Celts in Ireland, though there is a strong presumption that earlier settlements should be assigned to them.

The Decline of the Celts
In the early years of the third century the energy and resources of the Celts might have appeared inexhaustible. Masters of a vast area extending from Galatia in the east to Britain, and probably Ireland, in the west, they might have seemed ideally placed to establish an enduring empire or confederation. In the event, however, the Celts had reached the apogee of their

Carved stone pillar from Pfalzfeld in the Hunsrück. It is one of the earliest and most ornate of Celtic sculptures. Each of its four faces has a head with a huge two-leaved crown in the midst of stylised floral patterns. Originally the monument was surmounted by a head which was broken off in the seventeenth century. Rheinisches Landesmuseum, Bonn.

power, and thereafter they entered upon a period of rapid decline which in retrospect seems to have been almost inevitable. The very ease and extent of their conquests carried the seeds of their undoing. Distance weakened lines of communication and encouraged disintegration. In some areas the ruling Celts were a small minority in the midst of an indigenous population, while at the same time they squandered manpower on purely mercenary ventures.

In sum, the Celtic peoples lacked the sense of cohesion and the flair for centralised organisation that could have consolidated this scattering of tribes into an empire or commonwealth. Whether they would have developed these qualities, given time, is matter for pure speculation: in the event, they were soon pressed hard on several sides, in the north by the Germans, in the east by the Dacians,

and in the south by the Romans, and the end of the third century saw a steady recession of Celtic influence. A century later only fragments remained of their vast dominions, and the Celtic realm had come to be associated in a special sense with Gaul, where the Celts preserved their independence and separate identity until their conquest by Caesar.

Nor did this bring an end to their decline. In the first century B.C. Gaul was conquered by Caesar and incorporated within the Roman Empire,

---

The Gundestrup cauldron. This silver-plated copper bowl was discovered in 1891 in a peat bog at Gundestrup in Denmark and probably belongs to the first or second century B.C. It is richly decorated in high relief, on the outside with images of unidentified deities and on the inside with mythological scenes. It was obviously a cult cauldron. Nationalmuseet, Copenhagen.

and a century later the subjugation of Britain followed. When the Western Empire collapsed in the fifth century A.D. the Gaulish language was all but extinct: the language which continues to be spoken in Brittany is of different stock, having been introduced afresh by immigrations from south-west Britain during the fifth and six centuries. In Britain itself the Roman presence came to an end in the fifth century, only to be followed by that of the Anglo-Saxons, and from then on the area of Celtic speech and sovereignty was steadily reduced: today the British branch of Celtic survives only in Wales and in Brittany.

During this time Ireland enjoyed almost complete security from outside aggression, its inhabitants speaking a Celtic language, which linguists label Goidelic and which in its modern form is known as Gaelic. We know from Tacitus that the Roman

general Agricola intended it otherwise and claimed that the country could be taken and held by a single legion and a few auxiliaries. But Agricola's plan never came to fruition and Ireland suffered no major intrusion until the coming of the Vikings in the ninth century and the Anglo-Normans in the twelfth. Consequently, the Irish social order and the learned system which it maintained remained immune from violent assault until long after Ireland had become a Christian country and Irish a written language. This must be accounted one of the causes of the remarkable continuity and the conservative character of Irish learned tradition.

The Conservators of Tradition

It is clear that in the several Celtic areas for which we have evidence the cultivation of literature and learning, and in earlier times of religion, rested upon a highly organised system of professional classes. One gathers from Greek and Latin writers (whose information, as already noted, derives

The items on this page and on pages 12–13 are from a collection of wooden sculpture recovered recently from the marshes at the source of the Seine, in the vicinity of the Gallo-Roman sanctuary of Sequana. They include whole human figures, male and female, torsos, heads, limbs and internal organs, as well as animals. The sanctuary of Sequana, the goddess of the source, was evidently a therapeutic centre and doubtless many of these articles of sculpture were *ex voto* offerings to the deity. Musée Archéologique, Dijon.

Small bronze disc, evidently a pendant, 4 inches (10.5 cm) in diameter, from Loughan Island on the River Bann, Co. Antrim, first or second century A.D. The delicate curvilinear ornament consists essentially of a triskele with its constituent lines ending in small, crested birds' (ducks?) heads. Ulster Museum, Belfast.

Left. This bronze openwork object from Cornalaragh, Co. Monaghan, dates from the pre-Christian era, and is probably the lid of a cylindrical box. National Museum of Ireland, Dublin.

Below. The second side of the double stone figure on Boa Island, Co. Fermanagh (see page 131).

mainly from the Greek geographer Posidonius) that there were three such classes: the druids, the bards, and between them an order that is variously named in the several texts but which seems to have been best known by a Gaulish term *vātis,* cognate with Latin *vatis.* The druids had the highest social status, and even though their powers and functions may have been the subject of varying degrees of misrepresentation by writers from Julius Caesar to our day, their influence must nevertheless have been considerable. They officiated at sacrifices, made and enforced legal decisions, and conducted their own elaborate system of education. The *vates* are generally represented as experts in divination, but it is not possible to make any rigid distinction between their functions and those of the druids, and some would argue that they do not constitute a separate class but rather a subordinate division of the druidic order. The bards were the class primarily concerned with literature, and in view of the heroic character of Celtic society it is hardly surprising that classical sources should describe them principally as singers of praise-poetry.

This scheme of things, attested by classical authors, is substantially confirmed by Irish tradition. Again we find a threefold division, here comprising druids *(druïdh), filidh,* and bards *(baird).* As in the case of Gaul, here again it is difficult to distinguish rigorously between the intermediate class and the druids; indeed, already by the seventh century A.D. the *filidh* had become virtually the sole inheritors of such druidic functions and privileges as survived the stresses of the first few centuries of Christianity. Whereas the druids, as the foremost representatives of pagan religion, had borne the brunt of the Church's opposition until they finally disappeared as a distinct order, the *filidh* succeeded in establishing a remarkable *modus vivendi* with the ecclesiastical authorities which allowed the two bodies separate but complementary spheres of authority and permitted the *filidh* to continue many of their ancient functions and prerogatives, including some which had formerly belonged to the druids. Thus the *fil- idh,* whose title is often translated as 'poets', were in fact very much more: they were seers, teachers, advisers of rulers, witnesses of contracts, and down to the seventeenth century when the native order finally collapsed under the might of English government, their power of satire remained an effective social sanction.

But as poets they also extended their range of interest at the expense of the *baird.* The Irish bards were once closely associated with the composition of praise-poetry, like their counterparts in Gaul, but gradually the *filidh* expanded their own role until finally they could claim a virtual monopoly of this important social function. The status of the bards suffered and throughout most of Irish literary history they are presented as an inferior class of rhymers, storytellers and entertainers. In Wales, on the other hand, the term *bardd* survives with enhanced dignity into the historical period, being used as a general title for the learned poets who correspond to the Irish *filidh.*

Wooden sculpture recovered from the marshes at the source of the Seine, in the vicinity of the Gallo-Roman sanctuary of Sequana (see page 9).

The parallel between the Irish and Gaulish systems of learning is not merely one of titles and hierarchical status: it extends also to details of internal organisation and practice. According to Caesar the Gaulish druids were both teachers and disciples of learning: distrusting the written word, they memorised vast quantities of poetry, and some continued their studies for as much as twenty years. In Ireland the curriculum of the student *filidh* extended over a period of at least seven years; and for the rest, Caesar's observations are as relevant as for Gaul. He also says that the Gaulish druids had at their head one who held chief authority among them and that, at a certain fixed time of the year, they met in assembly at a holy place in the lands of the Carnutes which was regarded as the centre of Gaul. Similarly, the Irish druids, and their successors the *filidh*, had a leader elected from their own number, and they were closely associated in tradition with Uisnech, the 'navel' of Ireland, the location of the primal fire and reputedly the site of a great assembly *(mórdháil Uisnigh)*.

In its essentials the system was evidently pan-Celtic. The geographer Strabo (IV,4,4) implies as much, and other evidence confirms it. Druidism probably existed in Galatia as well as in Ireland, Britain and Gaul, and one of the key-words of religious ritual, *nemeton,* 'a sacred place', often used more particularly of a sacred grove, is attested in place-names throughout the Celtic world. Again from Strabo we learn that the council of the Galatians met in assembly at a place known as *drunemeton,* the 'oak-sanctuary' (XII,5,1), which is clearly analogous to the *locus consecratus,* 'consecrated place', where the Gaulish druids forgathered.

On a more general level one finds analogous institutions among several other peoples of the Indo-European linguistic group. The privileged priesthood of the druids had its counterpart in the Brahmans of India and the pontiffs of Rome, and it has been shown that these several priestly orders preserved elements of a common Indo-European religious terminology. What is still more important, they maintained, especially in the peripheral areas of India and Ireland, many cultural institutions and traditions bearing the unambiguous marks of a common origin. As late as the seventeenth century the Irish *filidh* continue usages which find their closest detailed parallel in the sacred texts of the Indian Brahmans: there could be no more eloquent testimony to the conservatism of Irish learned tradition.

The Sources
The earliest sources are those relating to the Celts of the continent – mainly Gaul – and of Romanised Britain. Unfortunately they have serious shortcomings. Gaulish literature, being purely oral, disappeared with the Gaulish language: we have it on Caesar's authority that the druids of Gaul considered it improper to commit their learning to writing, and on this point he is substantially borne out by the Irish evidence. As a result, since mythology implies narrative of some sort or other, Gaulish mythology, properly speaking, is lost beyond recovery. There remains, of course, a considerable body of residual evidence, but, since by its very nature it is allusive rather than descriptive, or else is reported at second hand, the modern student is frequently in the uncomfortable position of having to work from the ambiguous towards the unknown.

The evidence is of three types: dedi-

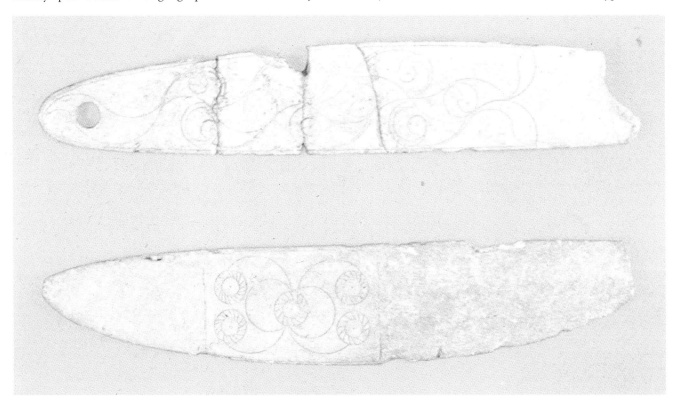

catory inscriptions such as occur throughout the territories occupied by the Romans, plastic representations of Celtic divinities, and observations by classical authors. In the first two categories the great bulk of the material belongs to the Roman period, and consequently it raises difficult problems of interpretation. For example, Gaulish sculpture developed under Greco-Roman influence and it is no easy task to determine precisely to what extent this influence may have affected the motifs of the sculpture as well as its form. As for the classical authors, it is a matter of scholarly opinion how much value should be placed upon their testimony. Most of them derive their information from earlier sources: even Caesar, who had a better opportunity than most to become acquainted with the Gaulish situation, is far from relying on his own experience and observation. And no doubt all of them were influenced to a greater or lesser degree by the forms and concepts of classical religion and mythology. These considerations have led some scholars to reject the classical evidence out of hand, which is probably an excess of scepticism. It should not be forgotten that a number of observations by the same classical authors on matters of Celtic custom and social organisation are corroborated by Irish literature: so closely in fact that certain early Irish tales might almost have been written to illustrate these comments on the continental Celts, and this few scholars would entertain as a serious possibility. The classical evidence therefore merits consideration, but it must be treated with extreme caution.

By way of contrast, the recorded testimony of Irish literature is later by a millennium or more, but, as we have seen, it has a conservative quality which more than outweighs the disparity in date. (The Irish language, despite the later date of its documents, seems in some respects to be more conservative than Gaulish, and the same may well hold true for the mythologies.) The writing down of Irish oral tradition had already commenced by the end of the sixth century, but time and the Viking raiders proved a ruthless combination and only a few manuscript fragments survive from the period before *c*.1100. Then comes the first of a number of great manuscript compilations which between them preserve a wealth of varied material relating to the Irish past. These manuscripts are themselves relatively late, but they have

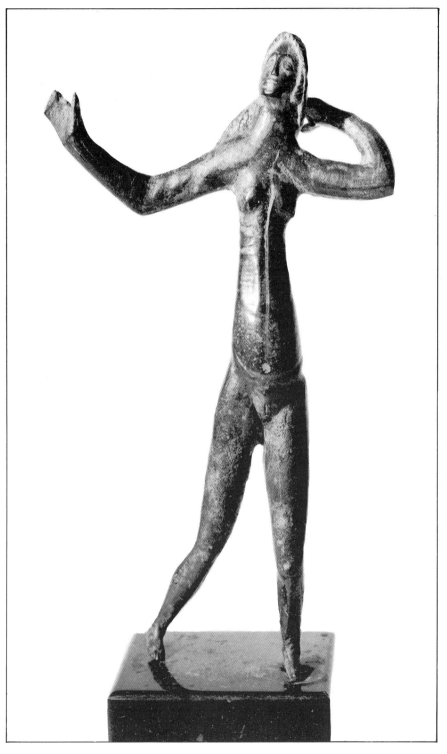

Opposite. Bone 'trial pieces' from Loughcrew, Co. Meath, perhaps late first century B.C. or first century A.D. These delicately engraved designs would evidently have been transferred later to metal objects. National Museum of Ireland, Dublin.

Right. Cast bronze statue of a girl dancing, from Neuvy-en-Sullias (Loiret), first century A.D. Musée Historique, Orléans.

been compiled from earlier sources and many of the individual items which they contain may be dated on linguistic grounds centuries earlier than their extant transcription. But, irrespective of their date of composition, it is beyond question that these texts contain a vast amount of pre-Christian matter.

Among the tales which formed an important part of the *filidh's* repertoire there are some which concern themselves explicitly with the supernatural world, and for that reason modern scholars sometimes refer to them as the Mythological Cycle. But this is a rather misleading title since in point of fact most early Irish narrative is mythological to a greater or lesser degree. There is much to be said for the native system of classification which groups the individual titles not by cycle but by theme: plunderings, cattle-raids, wooings, battles, voyages, adventures, elopements, etc. But for the sake of brevity the remaining tales may be divided into three broad categories: miscellaneous tales assigned to the reigns of various kings, historic and prehistoric (though this distinction has little relevance to the historicity of their content), the cycle of the Ulaidh or 'Ulstermen' with Conchobhar mac Nessa their king and Cú Chulainn their youthful hero, and finally the cycle of Fionn mac Cumhaill and the roving bands of warriors known as *fiana*.

The Ulster cycle was the literature of greatest prestige in the early period; it is heroic literature *par excellence* and it concerns itself with the activities and virtues that typify heroic society everywhere. By contrast, the Fionn cycle (or *fianaigheacht*, as it is often called) was more popular among the lower orders of society and correspondingly less highly esteemed by the *filidh*, and it is in fact only from the twelfth century, a watershed in Irish history and culture, that it bulks large in the literary record. Nevertheless, its roots lie deep in the pagan past. The great delight of the *fiana*, and their principal activity, is hunting, and this fact alone gives the cycle a quite different temper to that of the Ulster tales. It

is predominantly a literature of the open air that ranges far and wide throughout the changing landscape of Ireland, and in due course it becomes a convenient vehicle for numerous nature lyrics.

To this varied collection of tales one must add the pseudo-historical material, and in particular the *Leabhar Gabhála*, 'The Book of Invasions', and the *Dinnshenchas*, 'The History of Places'. The former is a twelfth-century compilation which purports to describe the several invasions of Ireland from the time of the Deluge (and even before it!). It is weak on history but relatively strong on myth. The *Dinnshenchas*, which also belongs to the twelfth century in its definitive form, is a massive collection of onomastic lore 'explaining' the names of well-known places throughout Ireland. Marie-Louise Sjoestedt has characterised the two rather neatly: *Leabhar Gabhála* is the mythological pre-history of the country and the *Dinnshenchas* its mythological geography.

There is enough evidence to indicate that Wales also inherited a rich mythological tradition, but, unfortunately, it is poorly documented. Like Ireland, Wales has its great manuscript compilations, the earliest of them from about the end of the twelfth century, but they do not preserve such a wealth of material from the early period as do the Irish counterparts. This is especially true of prose literature, and the earliest surviving tales, *Culhwch and Olwen* and *The Four Branches*, were probably first written in the eleventh century. The four tales, or 'branches', of the *Mabinogi* constitute one of the most important sources for British mythology. They abound in mythological themes and motifs and their *dramatis personae* are the ancient gods of Britain. Nevertheless, they represent the mere debris of a tradition recast in a loose narrative framework by a talented author who was less interested in preserving sources than in producing an effective piece of literature. There is also a considerable volume of mythological matter scattered through the remainder of medieval

literature, but clearly any semblance of an integrated mythological tradition had passed away long before the extant literature was recorded. What remains is an imbroglio of anecdotes, allusions, motifs and characters which under close scrutiny gradually reveal the outlines of a number of familiar mythological paradigms within a British setting.

The Welsh evidence derives a special interest from its close association with the great continental cycle of Arthurian romance. Welsh together with Breton literary tradition provided the many Celtic elements incorporated in the Arthurian romances of Chrétien de Troyes and his fellows, and not a little of the enduring fascination of these stories is due to their essentially mythological character. The original Arthur may well have been a historical person, but the King Arthur of medieval romance and his knightly entourage are much larger than life and share many of the mythological traits of the Irish hero Fionn mac Cumhaill and his *fiana*.

The Diversity of Celtic Mythology
To speak of 'Celtic mythology' is not to imply a close unity, but merely to recognise a tangible relationship based upon common inheritance. What we know of the mythology of the continental Celts hardly suggests a sustained correspondence with that of Ireland and Wales, and this cannot be due entirely to the unequal documentation. Even among the insular Celts the differences are, at first glance, much more evident than the underlying similarities. Nor is this very surprising, for a number of reasons: the several peoples in question do not derive from a single community of continental Celts; over the last two thousand years or more they have evolved somewhat differently in their social and cultural organisation; in the case of Britain and Gaul, but not of Ireland, they have been conditioned to the physical presence of Rome over a period of centuries; and, finally, it can safely be presumed that all assimilated much of the religious thought and usage of the pre-Celtic inhabitants of their several areas.

Two faces of the tricephalic head in siliceous sandstone from Corleck, Co. Cavan, of the first century A.D. There is a small hole in the base of the head, which suggests that it originally stood on a stone pillar or pedestal as did several continental heads. Another feature attested elsewhere is the small perforation in the narrow mouth of the front face: this is found also in at least two other Irish heads and in a number of British and continental examples, most notably that from Mšecké-Žehrovice in Czechoslovakia (see page 60). Triadic groupings are a common feature of Celtic myth and literature, and this conceptual image is abundantly reflected in the plastic arts of the continental Celts with their groups of three associated figures and single tricephalic figures. National Museum of Ireland, Dublin.

These considerations go far towards explaining the wide discrepancies between the three visible branches of Celtic mythology. But by themselves they are not sufficient to account for the lack of unity and order which is so evident within each separate branch. Instead, it has been argued that this incoherence simply reflects the decentralised structure of Celtic society, in which each tribe functioned as an independent political unit, the inference being that political autonomy was coupled with religious autonomy and that each

tribe had its own special gods, which might, or might not, be common to neighbouring tribes. It may be that this is in fact one of the causes of what has been described as 'the local and anarchical character' of Celtic mythology, though its effects may well be exaggerated by a defective documentation dating in all cases from a period of drastic readjustment, when native religious usage was exposed to the influence of systems of greater sophistication and prestige.

The Celts being notoriously rich in paradox, it is perhaps not surprising

to find that this local independence, which is such a feature of their political organisation, is in some respects counterbalanced by a highly developed sense of cultural affinity among the learned classes. Nowadays we know that what gave the Celts such unity as they possessed was not common racial origins but a common culture and environment. The classical ethnographers identified them – not infallibly it may be said – by their language, their shared characteristics, and their mode of life, as well as by their geographical location, and one can still sense something of this cultural coherence in the remarkable analogies, both of ideas and their expression, in the traditional literatures of Ireland and Wales. What is

even more to the point, the druidic order existed throughout the Celtic world and its organisation appears to have been essentially the same in all areas. The cult of the centre to which its members attached such importance epitomises their professional solidarity and their assiduous fostering of an ideological unity transcending the political divisions within each nation or agglomeration of tribes. This is a persistent trait and nowhere is it evidenced more clearly than in post-Norman Ireland where the *filidh* conserved an astonishing cultural unity in a world of political strife and instability.

This faculty for combining unity with diversity, centripetal with centrifugal forces, is no less evident in the mythology. Here the externals present a bewildering variety. The nomenclature continually renews itself even when the underlying concepts remain undisturbed. The myths proliferate in endless narrative variants but their themes are constant and, so far as one can judge, in large measure common to the whole Celtic world. For instance, the theme of divine sovereignty which is such a permanent and such a fundamental element of Irish tradition was also familiar in Britain and in Brittany, though most of the literature to which it gave rise there is known only from occasional allusions. It is this underlying homogeneity that justifies us in speaking of one Celtic mythology rather than of several.

Opposite. Bronze mask from Garancières-en-Beauce (Eure-et-Loir). The features are stylised in the Celtic manner, the hair swept back in parallel ridges. Musée des Beaux-Arts, Chartres.

Below. Janus heads in limestone from the sanctuary of Roqueperteuse near Aix-en-Provence, probably of the fourth century B.C. Directly below is a front view of one of them. These separate Janus heads, which must once have stood over a door or gateway, are divided by what some have identified as a horned crown but others as a great beak, perhaps that of a bird of prey. The sanctuary also has a portico furnished with niches for human skulls (see page 100). The site and its artifacts were probably influenced by the Ligurian subjects of the Celtic overlords around the Lower Rhone as well as by the Greek colony of Massilia (Marseilles), and Jabobsthal attributed the Janus heads to a Celtic sculptor who studied in Massilia. Musée Borély, Marseilles.

Gaulish Gods and Insular Equivalents

The Gods as Noted by Caesar

'Of the gods they worship Mercury most of all. He has the greatest number of images; they hold that he is the inventor of all the arts and a guide on the roads and on journeys, and they believe him the most influential for money-making and commerce. After him they honour Apollo, Mars, Jupiter, and Minerva. Of these deities they have almost the same idea as other peoples: Apollo drives away diseases, Minerva teaches the first principles of the arts and crafts, Jupiter rules the heavens and Mars controls the issue of war.' So runs Caesar's succinct description of the Gaulish pantheon. It illustrates admirably the Roman virtues of clarity and precision, and on that score alone it is open to suspicion. For these are not the salient virtues of Celtic mythology as it has been preserved, and when we turn to the evidence of dedications and sculpture – not to mention the insular Celtic literary tradition – we are faced with what appears to be a tangle of heterogeneous elements bearing little noticeable resemblance to Caesar's neat classification. Not merely does Caesar assign Roman names to the native gods, in accord with common practice in the ancient world, but he goes on to assert that the Gaulish conception of the deities so named differed little from that of other peoples, meaning in the first instance of course the Romans, and in this he is certainly not vindicated by the Celtic documents. In reality what Caesar gives us is a concise *interpretatio romana* of the facts as known to him; the abundance and variety of Gaulish mythology is reduced to a simple and convenient schema derived from that of Rome.

Caesar's account has been impugned on two main grounds: first, that it implies, erroneously, the existence of a pantheon of gods worshipped more or less universally throughout Gaul, and, secondly, that it enunciates a clear differentiation of divine functions for which there is no evidence in Celtic tradition. To note these twin objections is, in effect, to state the central problem of Celtic mythology.

It is frequently pointed out that of the numerous deity names attested in Gaulish dedications the great majority occur only once and that those which occur more often tend to be grouped within districts or regions. Many names have strictly local reference and some give explicit expression to the association between deity and tribal groupment, for instance *dea Brigantia* and *dea Tricoria*, the goddesses of the Brigantes and the Tricorii. And in the tales of the Ulster cycle several instances occur of an oath-formula which invokes 'the god of the tribe' – *tongu do dia toinges mo thuath* (variant: *toingte Ulaid*), 'I swear to the god to whom my tribe (or 'the Ulaidh') swear'. The French scholar Vendryes saw in this a neat illustration of the role of the Gaulish god *Teutates* mentioned by Lucan: a derivative of the Celtic word for tribe, *teutā*, his name would mean in effect 'the god of the tribe'.

In the light of such considerations as these it is easy to understand why so many commentators should have dwelt upon the multiplicity of the Celtic gods and the local character of their cults – Vendryes speaks of 'a nomenclature of local divinities' which reveals 'not even the trace of great divinities common to all the Celtic peoples'. But the result has

'Mercury' with his sacred animals: the
goat, the cock and the tortoise; from
Heddemheim (Frankfurt). Musée des
Antiquités Nationales, St Germain-en-
Laye.

been, one fears, to exaggerate the 'anarchical' aspect of the mythology and in the same measure to obscure rather than to elucidate its essential structure.

In the first place there is the matter of the Gaulish names in the dedications. In many cases these names are attached, whether as nouns or adjectives, to names of Roman deities; in other words, they are the visible marks of a syncretism whose very existence implies a certain disorientation of Gaulish religion at the time and whose effects are difficult to assess accurately in any particular instance. For example, does a dedication to Mars Vesontius mean simply that the Roman god was venerated in the region of Besançon, or that an unnamed god of extensive cult and equated with Mars was venerated there, or finally, as Vendryes and others would assume, that a local indigenous god was equated with Mars? In fact we know that a multiplicity of names does not necessarily imply a multiplicity of deities, and insular Celtic tradition provides many instances of important deities known by several different names. And while it is clear beyond question that the Celts placed strong emphasis upon the local and tribal affiliations of their gods, it does not follow that they lacked gods of wider significance and cult: only by a prodigious stretch of the imagination could one conceive of the insular gods Lugh, the Daghdha and Mabon/mac ind Óg as local deities.

It has also been argued that there is no separation of divine functions such as indicated by Caesar. In the view of some who propose this argument there existed – apart from the goddesses – tribal gods who were more or less polyvalent, in other words who commanded a more or less wide range of functions, and they see no reason to suppose that each of these was assigned a distinct sphere of human activity as were the gods of Rome. Others of them hold that the

many mythical personages attested in archaeological records and in literary tradition may be reduced to an ultimate unity, since they are all variant manifestations of a single supreme deity, in itself indefinite, impersonal, polyvalent and polymorphic. T. F. O'Rahilly, the principal exponent of this view, constructed his interpretation of Irish mythology around the central idea of a mythic conflict in which this great lord of the otherworld was slain by a youthful hero, using the god's own sacred weapon, the thunderbolt.

It is true that certain features of the evidence lend themselves to such a theory of a single great deity appearing under various forms and titles. One finds, for example, that different deities perform similar functions and that sharply differentiated 'departmental' gods in the classical sense are here conspicuous rather by their absence. One finds also that in different contexts any one of several deities may be accorded apparent primacy or represented as presiding over the Otherworld Feast. But it is not as yet clear to what extent, if at all, this implies a predisposition to monotheism. Indeed one cannot but reflect that if the Celts were monotheists at heart, then they were remarkably

successful in disguising this, for not merely have they fractured their single godhead into a multiplicity of aliases, but they have also invested some of these with a convincing air of individuality. It may be expected, moreover, that such a latent or implicit monotheism would have been at some earlier period palpable and explicit, but the evidence of Indian and other Indo-European mythologies makes this seem unlikely. Furthermore, it may be recalled that the two notions of Celtic divinity referred to here, the one polytheistic and the other vaguely monotheistic, begin with the same basic assumption, namely that the Celtic gods were universally competent, or polyvalent, and this is something which cannot be accepted without very considerable qualification. For, as we shall see presently, there are insular deities –

Goibhniu the smith and Dian Cécht the leech are the most conspicuous examples – who were credited with clearly defined central functions, and, as for the rest, it is at least clear that their spheres of activity are far from being identical. In point of fact, more recent studies in the field – notably those of Françoise Le Roux and Anne Ross – place increasing emphasis on the functional grouping of the several deities and it seems that their ultimate classification must be a typological one, with functional emphasis as the primary criterion. Certainly nomenclature alone is a poor guide to the number of Celtic gods and the extension of cults.

This has an obvious relevance to Caesar's account. For in so far as he implies the existence of a pantheon of specifically titled gods known and revered throughout the length and

breadth of Gaul, he is palpably in error. But if, on the other hand, his pantheon was intended as a typological index rather than as a list of individual deities, then it may be relatively close to the realities of the Gaulish situation: the very fact that 'Mercury' ranks first in his hierarchy and 'Jupiter' only fourth shows that his *interpretatio romana* was not a purely mechanical one.

Gaulish 'Mercury': Irish Lugh

According to Caesar the Gauls regarded Mercury 'as the inventor of all the arts and a guide on the roads and on journeys . . . and the most influential for money-making and commerce.' The resemblance to the Roman Mercury is obvious, though the Gaulish god is credited with somewhat wider interests. That he was in fact the most honoured of the gods seems to be confirmed by the archaeological evidence. His inscriptions and monuments are more numerous than those of any other god, so that Caesar evidently spoke truly when he reported that *huius sunt plurima simulacra* (the images of this god are very many). The wide range of his cult is attested by modern placenames and its tenacity by references in saints' lives to the destruction of his temples and statues by missionary saints. His images frequently assimilate him to the classical Mercury: youthful, beardless, equipped with caduceus, petasus and purse, and accompanied by cock, goat (ram) or tortoise. But he also occurs bearded and dressed in Gaulish fashion, and he is often associated with a goddess who is named 'Maia' or Rosmerta and who evidently represents wealth and material abundance. Unlike his classical counterpart, his arts include that of war.

The native name of the Gaulish Mercury has nowhere been recorded. But for this fact it might have been possible to speak unreservedly of a pre-eminent deity known throughout the Celtic world; for even without the

Mercury carrying caduceus and purse. Landesmuseum, Stuttgart.

conclusive evidence of a shared title it is commonly accepted that 'Mercury' and the Irish god Lugh are one. And indeed the arguments for such an identification are impressive. In the first place Caesar's phrase *omnium inventorem artium* might almost be a gloss on Lugh's soubriquet, *(sam)ildánach*, 'possessing, or skilled in many arts (together)', which is explained in the tale of the battle of Magh Tuiredh by the fact that Lugh commanded all the arts possessed severally by the many craftsmen in the house of Nuadha, king of the Tuatha Dé Danann, the divine people of Irish tradition. Lugh, we are told, came to the royal court of Tara while a great feast was in progress. The doorkeeper asked what skill he possessed, since no one without a special skill might enter Tara. 'I am a wright', said Lugh. 'We do not require you; we have a wright already.' 'I am a smith', said Lugh. But the doorkeeper replied that they had one. And so Lugh continued his catalogue of skills – as champion, harper, hero, poet-historian, sorcerer, leech, cupbearer, craftsman in metal – only to be told that the Tuatha Dé Danann already had experts in these. He then asked whether they had any one person who combined all these skills. Naturally they had not, and Lugh was permitted to enter. Elsewhere in the same text Lugh is referred to as the inventor of *fidhchell* (the classic boardgame of Irish tradition), ball-play and horsemanship.

Moreover, Lugh's cult was not confined to Ireland. It is, for example, implicit in the placename *Lugudunon*, Latin *Lugudunum*, which includes his name in its older form *Lugus* and from which derive – among other modern names – Lyon and Laon in France, Leiden in Holland and Leignitz in Silesia. The Romano-British name of the modern Carlisle in the north of England was *Luguvalium* (or *Luguvallum*), which Professor Jackson derives from British *Luguvalos* meaning 'He who is strong like (the god) Lugus' or 'Strong in (the god) Lugus'. The town of Lyon, whose name commemorates its association with Lugus, was chosen by Augustus as the capital of Gaul

and the site of his own annual festival, to be held on 1 August. This obviously continued an older Celtic festival dedicated to the town's divine patron, and it is significant that on this day was celebrated, and indeed still is celebrated, throughout Ireland the feast of Lughnasadh, 'commemoration of Lugh'.

The Welsh cognate of Lugh is Lleu who in one incident in the tale of *Math vab Mathonwy* is made briefly to assume the guise of a shoemaker. It has been suggested that this incident may be related to an inscription found at Osma in Spain which bears a dedication to the *Lugoves* (plural of *Lugus*) on behalf of a *collegium sutorum* (guild of shoemakers). These Lugoves, who recur in an inscription from Avenches in Switzerland, are probably an instance of triplication of the deity which is a familiar feature of Celtic mythology. Finally, there is the interesting coincidence that Lugh's festival is in Ireland often celebrated on hill-tops while in Gaul Mercury's cult was associated with a number of elevated sites, such as the Puy-de-Dôme where the Arverni had one of the largest statues of the ancient world erected in his honour.

Lugh, whose name means 'The Shining One', is in fact the most colourful figure among the divine Tuatha Dé Danann. Youthful, athletic and handsome, he appears as victor over malevolent otherworld beings, as king of the Tuatha Dé Danann after Nuadha and as divine father of the great hero Cú Chulainn. He possesses a marvellous spear, though it is with a sling-shot that he kills his greatest antagonist, Balar of the baleful eye. Lughnasadh, his feast, is a harvest festival. Two of its principal sites, Carmun and Tailtiu, and probably others besides, were the burial places of female deities who are clearly associated with the earth and its fertility. He is the 'divine prototype of human kingship', and it is told that when Conn 'of the Hundred Battles', famous king of Tara, visited Lugh he found him seated in state as a king of the otherworld and attended by a young and regally dressed woman who is clearly identified as

the sovereignty of Ireland. This personification of the land of Ireland – and of her sub-divisions – is one of the most persistent themes in Irish tradition, and this particular instance where the goddess who represents the land and its prosperity is coupled with Lugh can scarcely be dissociated from the Gaulish monuments to Mercury and Rosmerta.

It has been suggested more than once that Lugh is a relatively late arrival among the Celtic gods, but this is unlikely. It is true that he appears in the literature as a newcomer to the Tuatha Dé Danann, but one cannot assume that this reflects a *historical* process. And the fact that he is noted for his innovations does not mean necessarily that he himself is one. Not only is it virtually certain that he was known to all the Celtic peoples, but he is analogous in several respects, notably in his use of magic, to the Germanic Odin and the Indian Varuna. His usual epithet, *Lámhfhada*, 'of the long arm', has been taken to refer to his mode of fighting (with throwing spear and sling), or compared with the similar epithet of the Indian god Savitar, 'of the wide hand', who stretches out his hand to control sun, moon and stars and to regulate the succession of day and night. But the most likely view is that Lugh's epithet reflects the traditional concept of kingship which he himself personifies in the literature and that it may even be read as a kind of gloss on the Celtic word for 'king': Irish *rí*, like Latin *rēx* and Sanskrit *rāj-*, evidently derives from an old Indo-European verb meaning 'to stretch out' (the hand etc.), then 'to protect', and finally 'to rule', thus providing a neat compendium of the historical evolution of ancient tribal kingship. Even if other evidence were lacking, his epithet alone would almost be sufficient to confirm Lugh's origins in the Celts' Indo-European heritage.

Teutates, Esus, Taranis: 'Mars', 'Jupiter'

In the first century A.D., Lucan mentions three deities by their Gaulish names (*De Bello Civili* I, 444-6): 'Cruel Teutates propitiated by bloody

sacrifice, and uncouth Esus of the barbarous altars, and Taranis whose altar is no more benign than that of Scythian Diana'. He is evidently bent on titillating his metropolitan public at the expense of the Gauls, and one must allow for considerable exaggeration and misplaced emphasis. However, his mention of the cruel sacrifices by which these gods were appeased is taken up and expanded by a commentator writing centuries later, and these additions have generated much scholarly discussion and many conflicting theories.

According to one of the sources cited by the later writer the victims of Teutates were asphyxiated by being plunged head foremost into a full vat, those of Esus were suspended from trees and ritually wounded, and those of Taranis were burned, numbers of them together in cages of wood. Obviously these details were not invented by the commentator, but one cannot be sure that he cites them in their true context. The sacrifice to Taranis echoes Posidonius (as followed by Caesar and others), who reported in the first century B.C. that the Gauls burned numbers of human victims in huge wicker-work images. The sacrifice to Esus is not clearly defined, but it may be the remnant of a myth similar to that of the Germanic Odin who hung on the World Tree for nine days and nine nights and whose victims were likewise left hanging on trees.

The account of the Teutates rite recalls a scene pictured on the famous Gundestrup cauldron (see page 28), but the connection once assumed has latterly been called in question. It has also been compared with the death by drowning in a vat of mead, beer or wine which is ascribed by legend to the two Irish kings Diarmaid mac Cerbhaill and Muirchertach mac Erca as well as to the Norse Fjölnir. In the Irish legends the king is wounded, the house in which he is trapped burned down about him, and he finally perishes in a vat of liquor while attempting to escape from the flames. The fact that this elaborately contrived death takes place at Samhain, the sacred festival marking the end of summer, suggests that we have to do here with a recurrent mythological theme and, more specifically, with a rite relating to the sacred kingship. At the same time, it is to be noted that these Irish narratives belong to the well-known motif of the Threefold Death in which a person fulfils an unlikely prophecy by suffering three different

Opposite. 'Jupiter' from the Paris monument which also bears reliefs of Esus and Tarvos Trigaranus. Musée de Cluny, Paris.

Below. The god Mars as he appears on a square buttress from Paris. Though 'Mars' is frequently furnished with Gaulish epithets or sobriquets, his appearance is always that of the Roman deity. Musée de Cluny, Paris.

deaths, in these cases by wounding, burning and drowning. The exact relationship between the international motif and the rite or rites recorded by the commentator of Lucan therefore remains to be explained.

The commentator's two main sources disagree about the Roman equivalent of Teutates, the one equating him with Mercury, the other with Mars. These late identifications are probably without significance, but it does happen to be true that the Gaulish Mars and Mercury tended to be assimilated and their functions to overlap. Thus we find the epithets *Iovantucarus* and *Vellaunus* applied to both deities. And just as Mercury-Lugh is a god of warrior prowess as well as of arts and crafts, so, despite Caesar, the Mars of Gaulish inscriptions is more than a god of war: he is a god of healing, fertility and protection, the guardian of his people

and of their material prosperity whether against disease or against hostile arms. It is not surprising, therefore, that on some inscriptions he is qualified as Teutates, that is to say, as the tutelary god of the tribe: as already remarked, *teutates* appears originally to have been a descriptive term rather than a proper name, though it may well have evolved towards the latter.

Esus figures in the guise of a wood-cutter on two reliefs of the first century A.D. (see pages 29 and 33), but while these are of great interest and must reflect some episode from myth, unfortunately they lend themselves to an inordinately wide range of interpretations. It is difficult to estimate how widespread was his cult; his name occurs for certain in only one inscription.

For Taranis the evidence is a little more substantial. His title designates

him as the 'Thunderer', and in several dedications he is expressly identified with Jupiter. The particularly Celtic attributes of this Gallo-Roman Jupiter are his wheel, which may be either a lightning or a solar symbol, and, less frequently, the spiral which represents the lightning flash. Wherever we find this god – and he is attested throughout the Romano-Celtic area – it seems reasonable to equate him with the god known as Taranis.

It does not follow, however, that he was universally known by this particular name; in fact it is unattested as a proper name in Irish, while Welsh has only two instances which are of uncertain relevance. Neither can it be said that insular tradition retains any clear reflection of such an individualised god. Irish deities are commonly assigned marvellous weapons and these have sometimes been regarded as symbolising the

divine thunderbolt, but even if this were justified, the fact remains that these Otherworld arms are not the attribute of any single god. On the other hand, the Irish evidently set great store by the power of the elements. Solemn oaths are sworn under the sanction of sun and moon, water and air, etc., and are followed by swift retribution if violated.

In the great saga of *Táin Bó Cuailnge* (The Cattle-Raid of Cuailnge), when the Ulstermen are rebuked by the severed head of Sualtaimh for their tardiness in coming to the support of the hero Cú Chulainn as he stands alone in defence of the province, Conchobhar their king makes this reply: 'A little too loud is that cry, for the sky is above us, the earth beneath us and the sea all around us, but unless the sky with its showers of stars fall upon the surface of the earth or unless the ground burst open in an earthquake, or unless the fish-abounding, blue-bordered sea come over the surface of the earth, I shall bring back every cow to its byre and enclosure, every woman to her own abode and

Opposite. In this scene from the interior of the Gundestrup cauldron a man is plunged head foremost into a vat by a larger figure, presumably a deity. On the right a line of foot-soldiers advances towards the deity, while above them mounted soldiers ride off in the opposite direction preceded by a ram-headed serpent. This composition lends itself to various interpretations. Some authors explain it by reference to an early testimony which states that victims were sacrificed to Teutates by being drowned in a vat; the large figure would thus be the god Teutates. Others interpret it as a resurrection scene centred upon the 'cauldron of immortality', while Jan de Vries prefers to regard it as representing an initiation ceremony. Nationalmuseet, Copenhagen.

Below. Reliefs from a pillar dedicated to Jupiter by the 'Parisian mariners' between A.D. 14 and 37 and rediscovered in 1711 under the choir of the cathedral of Nôtre Dame in Paris. One shows the god Esus cutting branches from a tree. In the other there is a similar tree with a bull surmounted by three birds. It bears the title *Tarvos Trigaranus*, 'The Bull with the Three Cranes'. That these two adjacent scenes belong together is confirmed by a relief from Trèves (see page 33) in which a man, similarly dressed in short working tunic, appears to be hacking the trunk of a tree in whose foliage are visible the head of a bull and the same three birds. These three components, the tree, the bull and the otherworld birds, are familiar features of insular Celtic tradition, and obviously we have to do here with some episode from a myth. Unfortunately its precise content can only be conjectured. Musée de Cluny, Paris.

dwelling, after victory in battle and combat and contest.' The mentality here revealed is of great antiquity: it is, for example, that of the Adriatic Celts who, when they were asked by Alexander the Great what they feared most, are reported to have said – with a disarming candour – that they feared no one, unless it were that the sky might fall upon them.

Gaulish 'Apollo' and Congeners

Like the classical god with whom he is equated in Gallo-Roman sources and by Caesar, the Gaulish Apollo 'drives away diseases'. In particular, he is the patron deity of thermal springs. His dedications are more numerous than the status of his Roman counterpart would warrant and it is obvious that the gods assimilated to the classical deity enjoyed an extensive and popular cult.

One may use the plural here with fair confidence, for of the fifteen or more epithets applied to 'Apollo' in Gaulish inscriptions there are several which occur relatively frequently and are evidently separate deity names. The commonest of these, *Belenus*, is attested – often alone – in the old Celtic kingdom of Noricum in the eastern Alps, of which according to Tertullian he was the special deity, as well as in northern Italy and southern Gaul, and there are also traces of his cult in Britain. It recalls the Irish name for May-day, *Beltene*, of which the second element, *tene*, is the word

for 'fire' and the first, *bel*, probably means 'shining, brilliant'. This, together with the fact that he is equated with Apollo, suggests that Belenus had a markedly solar character. In fact the same probably holds true for the Gaulish Apollo in general: his connection with thermal springs argues as much, and one of his epithets, *Atepomāros*, 'possessing a great horse, great horses', seems to contain a common solar symbolism.

But this is to raise an old and vexed problem among the Celts. The *locus classicus* for this is the passage of St Patrick's *Confession* in which he contrasts worship of the sun, which rises by the command of God, with worship of the true Sun which is Christ, the one leading to pain and damnation, the other to eternal life. This is sometimes taken to constitute clear proof of the existence of sun-worship

in Ireland, but it is more likely to be one of the theological commonplaces acquired by Patrick through his religious reading and training. And if one excludes this, then in all the substantial remains of Irish tradition there is hardly any worthwhile evidence for a cult of the sun. There is, it is true, an abundance of solar symbolism, or motifs which lend themselves to such an interpretation, and there are gods who, like the Gaulish Apollo, are associated with attributes of the sun; but one can scarcely speak of sun-worship as such without doing violence to the extant traditions of Ireland and Wales.

Another name for 'Apollo', *Grannus*, awaits a satisfactory etymology, but we know that the god so named was credited with curative powers, and according to Dio Cassius he was invoked by the emperor Caracalla in

A.D. 215, together with Aesculapius and Serapis. He is usually paired with the goddess *Sirona*, whose title is derived from a word for 'star'.

Borvo (Bormo, Bormanus) is the Gaulish deity most closely associated with thermal waters. His name denotes boiling or seething water and is preserved in a number of placenames, including Bourbonne-les-Bains. His female companion is *Damona*, 'The Divine Cow'.

The cult of *Maponos*, 'The Divine Youth (Son)', is attested principally in the north of Britain, but it existed also in Gaul, in the vicinity of healing springs. In Britain he was evidently credited with skill in the art of music – he is at least once equated with Apollo *Citharoedus*, 'the Harper' – but this conception of deities as poet-musicians is not uncommon among the insular Celts. He appears in Welsh literature as Mabon son of Modron, that is to say, son of *Matrona*, 'The Divine Mother', eponymous goddess of the river Marne in France. In the tale of *Culhwch and Olwen* Mabon pursues the magic boar called the Twrch Trwyth and retrieves from between its ears the razor required by Culhwch. But first Culhwch had to deliver him from the captivity in which he had been held at Caer Loyw (Gloucester, but here obviously a designation for the otherworld) since he was taken away from his mother when three nights old. These references serve to confirm other indications that in Britain Maponos was known as a hunter, but unfortunately they offer only a tantalising glimpse of his myth. He survives in continental Arthurian romance under the names Mabon, Mabuz and Mabonagrain.

In Ireland the obvious parallel to Mabon-Maponos is *Mac ind Óg,* 'The Young Lad', also known as *Oenghus.* His father is the Daghdha, chief god of the Irish, and his mother is Boann, wife of Nechtan (originally a water-deity) and eponym of the great river of Irish mythology. In order to conceal their illicit union from the divine Elcmhaire who has undertaken to return by nightfall, Boann and the Daghdha cause the sun to stand still for a full nine months, so that Oenghus is conceived and born on the same day. Later Irish romances tend to portray Oenghus as something of a wilful and witty trickster and this need not be entirely an innovation: early tales tell how by means of a verbal ruse he took permanent possession of the supernatural dwelling of Bruigh na Bóinne from his father the Daghdha or from Elcmhaire. In *Aislinge Oenguso,* 'The Dream of Oenghus', he is the lover wasted by longing for a girl he has seen only in a dream. After a prolonged search throughout Ireland the girl is found and the tale ends with the lovers flying off to Bruigh na Bóinne in the form of a pair of swans and chanting such a wondrous music that all who heard it slept for three days and nights.

On the other hand, Mac ind Óg has no obvious connection with healing; this is the special function of *Dian Cécht,* one of the craft-gods of the Tuatha Dé Danann. He it was who, when Nuadhu the king lost his arm in conflict, replaced it with a silver one, and also restored the slain to life in the second battle of Magh Tuiredh, the paramount battle of Irish mythological tradition. It has been argued that Dian Cécht shows certain solar features, which would of course bring him closer to the Gaulish Apollo, but there is little to connect him with the cult of healing springs which characterises the Gaulish deity. He appears rather as the divine leech who effects his cures through a happy blend of therapeutic herbs and magic. According to *The Battle of Magh Tuiredh* he sang incantations over a well into which he then cast the mortally wounded so that they arose again as whole as ever, but whether this is sufficient to identify him as a god of healing springs is open to question. The cult of wells is, of course, ancient and well attested among the insular Celts and is reflected in the great number of 'holy wells' frequented until recent times in Ireland, and even in Wales, but it is not easy to link the therapeutic virtues of these wells with any particular deity.

One fact that emerges clearly from the insular evidence is that Mabon and Mac ind Óg on the one hand and Dian Cécht on the other embody only certain of the aspects or functions which in Gaul are subsumed under the portmanteau title of 'Apollo', and the same probably holds true of the several native deities identified with him in Romano-Gaulish inscriptions. It would be as foolish to equate Maponos with Borvo as to equate Mac ind Óg with Dian Cécht.

Gaulish 'Minerva': Irish Brighid

'Minerva' belongs to the numerous class of mother-goddesses whose role is so very fundamental to Celtic mythology – one of her epithets, *Sulevia,* occurs in the plural *Suleviae* as a title

for the 'mothers' both on the continent and in Britain. It is not without reason, therefore, that Caesar includes 'Minerva' among the major deities of Gaul. One cannot, of course, be certain whether he had in mind the whole class of such goddesses or a single representative, but if the former, then his description of 'Minerva' as a patron of arts and crafts does not give an adequate idea of the complex and far-reaching functions of the female deities nor their all-pervasive influence in the religious thought of the Celtic peoples. It may be that he identified the Gaulish Minerva too closely with her classical counterpart.

In her capacity as patron of arts and crafts, 'Minerva' figures on a number of reliefs together with Mercury and Vulcan, a grouping which

– like the pre-eminence of Mercury-Lugh – underlines the great prestige of the technical skills in early Celtic society. The dedications show that her cult was especially strong among the lower social orders, and as patron of the domestic arts her memory survives in the admonition of St Eligius (seventh century) not to invoke Minerva when engaged in weaving, dyeing or other such tasks. As patron of the art of healing she was honoured at thermal springs; at Bath (*Aquae Sulis*) she was assimilated to the native deity Sulis who had been worshipped there.

Her nearest counterpart in insular tradition is the goddess *Brighid*, of whom it is said in Cormac's Glossary (*c*.900) that she was expert in *fili-dhecht*, in other words poetry and traditional learning in general as well

Above. The relief from Trèves which corresponds to the Paris relief of Esus and Tarvos Trigaranus. It shows a woodcutter attacking a tree on which repose three birds and the head of a bull. Landesmuseum, Trier.

Above left. Bronze figure of the Gallo-Roman Jupiter, from Châtelet (Haute-Marne). As well as the Greco-Roman thunderbolt, he carries the Celtic spiral-symbol and his left hand rests upon the wheel which is the emblem of the Celtic Taranis, 'The Thunderer'. Musée des Antiquités Nationales, St Germain-en-Laye.

Opposite left. It has been suggested that this Celtic-style head from Corbridge (Corstopitum), Northumberland, represents the god Maponos, but this is not certain. It has a hollow on top for libations. Museum of Antiquities, Newcastle upon Tyne.

Opposite right. Relief of Minerva from Lower Slaughter, Gloucestershire. Gloucester Museum.

as divination and prophecy, and was worshipped by the *filidh*. By the same account she was daughter of the Daghdha and had two sisters also named Brighid, the one associated with healing and the other with the smith's craft, and from their common name 'among all the Irish a goddess used to be called Brighid'. As regards function, therefore, Brighid was patron of poetry and learning, of healing and of craftsmanship, and, as regards status, such was her prestige that her name could be used as a synonym for 'goddess'.

But paradoxically, it is in the person of her Christian namesake St Brighid that the pagan goddess survives best. For if the historical element in the legend of St Brighid is slight, the mythological element is correspondingly extensive, and it is clear beyond question that the saint has usurped the role of the goddess and much of her mythological tradition.

The saint's *Life* infers a close connection with livestock and the produce of the earth. Appropriately, her feast-day, 1 February, coincides with *Imbolg*, the pagan festival of spring; even today it is still the occasion of various popular and patently un-Christian rituals. She was born, we are told, at sunrise neither within nor without a house, is fed from the milk of a white, red-eared cow (that is, by Irish usage, a supernatural cow), hangs her wet cloak on the rays of

the sun, and the house in which she is staying appears to the onlookers to be all ablaze. According to Giraldus Cambrensis she and nineteen of her nuns took turns in guarding a sacred fire which burned perpetually and was surrounded by a hedge within which no male might enter. In this Brighid is evidently at one with 'Minerva', for we have it on the authority of Solinus writing in the third century that Minerva's sanctuary in Britain also contained a perpetual fire (a circumstance which may possibly have a bearing on Minerva's epithet *Belisama*, 'Most Brilliant').

It must be accepted, therefore, that no clear distinction can be made between the goddess and the saint and that in all probability Brighid's great monastery of Kildare was formerly a pagan sanctuary. It is indeed significant that, while Brighid was not a missionary saint nor widely travelled, yet in Ireland she was second only to Patrick in popular favour and dedications to her are found throughout the territories of the insular Celts, so that one can scarcely avoid the conclusion that her widespread cult substantially continues that of her pagan predecessor.

In point of fact the latter also can be traced throughout the Celtic area. The name Brighid was originally an epithet meaning 'the exalted one', just as its cognate *brihatī* was used as a divine epithet in Vedic Sanskrit, and this perhaps gives point to Cormac's remark quoted above that 'among all the Irish a goddess used to be called Brighid'. It had a close correspondent in the British *Brigantī*, latinised as *Brigantia*, 'the exalted one', tutelary goddess of the Brigantes. If, as seems not improbable, the tribe takes its name from the goddess, then she must also have been known on the continent whence they migrated and where some of them remained. Like Boann and Matrona and other Celtic goddesses, she gives her name to rivers: the Brighid in Ireland, the Braint in Wales and the Brent in England. Clearly, therefore, Brighid-Brigantia has strong claims to be equated with Caesar's Minerva. She is, at all events, one of the chief Celtic goddesses.

Gaulish 'Vulcan': Irish Goibhniu, Welsh Gofannon

That the smith was a person of consequence in Celtic society is clear from the laws and literature of the insular Celts, and indeed something of his special social status survived in rural Ireland until the decline of the craft in recent times. In particular, he has always carried a certain aura of supernatural competence: an eighth-century hymn which invokes God's aid 'against the spells of women and smiths and druids' presents a jaundiced ecclesiastical view of this peculiar faculty and no doubt runs counter to general contemporary attitudes. Perhaps a better guide to these attitudes would be the nineteenth-century countryman's high regard for the smith's charms and spells, so readily and frequently placed at his disposal, and especially for his powers of healing – by natural and supernatural means. The smith's prestige may be due partly to the nature of the craft, which affected almost all the essential activities of pre-modern society, in peace and in war, and partly perhaps to the close association with the magic properties of iron. At the same time, it cannot be divorced, whether as cause or effect, from the Celtic conception of the divine smith.

Caesar does not mention a Gaulish Vulcan, which is an oversight on his part, since this deity is otherwise well attested and in fact appears to have enjoyed a higher dignity than his Roman counterpart. His name has not survived, but it was very probably related to the forms which occur in the insular tradition. In Ireland the divine smith was known as *Goibhniu* and in Wales as *Gofannon*, both derived from the word for 'smith'. Goibhniu is the first of a triad of craftsman-gods, the others being *Luchta* (or *Luchtaine*) the wright and *Creidhne* the worker in metal. In the great battle of Magh Tuiredh they provide weapons for Lugh and the Tuatha Dé Danann, Goibhniu forging the heads, Luchta fashioning the shafts and Creidhne the rivets, and between them they form a divine assembly-line of dazzling speed and precision. And furthermore, every weapon of Goibhniu's manufacture carries a guarantee that it will never make an erring cast and that no one whom it wounds will survive.

Like his human successors of recent times, Goibhniu was evidently known for his therapeutic powers, for he is invoked in an Old Irish charm for the removal of a thorn. But his most significant attribute is his role as host or provider of the Otherworld feast known as *Fledh Ghoibhnenn*, 'The Feast of Goibhniu'. Those who partook of it were rendered exempt from age and decay: in other words they became immortal. The staple of this feast was an intoxicating drink corresponding to the *amrita* of Indian tradition and to analogous beverages of the gods. In the *Iliad* Hephaestos, Goibhniu's counterpart, is also made to serve the gods with drink, though there is nothing to show that this is one of the functions peculiar to him, and, to come nearer home, there may be a trace of the old mythology in the curious stipulation of the Welsh laws which says that the smith of the court shall have the first drink of the feast.

As host of the Otherworld feast Goibhniu was obviously considered one of the greater deities, but it is in his capacity as divine craftsman that he caught, and held, the imagination of the Irish people. Under the title of *Gobbán Saer*, 'Gobbán the Wright', he was already renowned as a wondrous builder in the earliest period of written Irish literature, and under the modern form, *an Gobán Saor*, he is remembered affectionately in folktales as the master of all masons who bests rivals and enemies by his ready wit and resource.

Gaulish Ogmios-Hercules: Irish Oghma

According to Lucian, who wrote during the second century A.D., Hercules was known to the Celts as *Ogmios*. He describes a Gaulish picture of him armed with his familiar club and bow but portrayed uncharacteristically as an old man, bald and grey, with skin darkened and wrinkled by the sun, more like Charon than Hercules, and drawing behind him a joyful band of men attached to him by thin chains

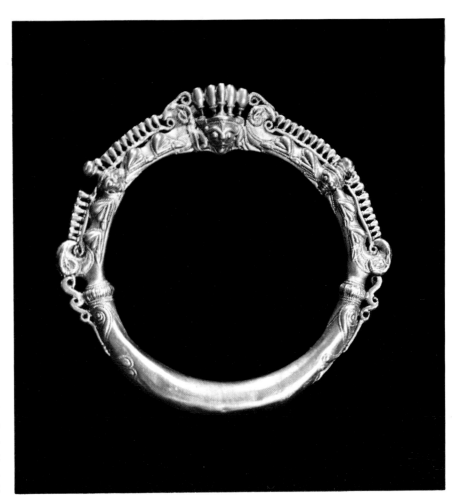

which linked their ears to the tip of his tongue. By way of elucidation, Lucian quotes a Gaulish informant who explained that his fellow Celts did not identify eloquence with Hermes, as did the Greeks, but rather with Hercules because he was much the stronger. The existence of Ogmios is further confirmed by two *defixiones*, inscribed tablets on which he is besought to wreak a curse on certain individuals.

If these few materials are to yield anything of their original total significance, it seems essential that they be considered in conjunction with the Irish traditions of the god Oghma, sometimes qualified as *grianainech*, 'of the sun-like countenance'. It is not at all certain that the form *Oghma* is the regular Irish reflex of a Celtic *Ogmios*, but, nevertheless, the consensus of opinion is that the two names must be identified in terms of mythology and some have resolved the linguistic problem by assuming that Oghma is a borrowing from Gaulish *Ogmios*

Above. Gold bracelet from Rodenbach, Rheinfalz. It is decorated with Janus heads flanked by crouching rams with eagle-beaks. Historisches Museum der Pfalz, Speyer.

Opposite. The Gaulish Hercules who was evidently identical with the god Ogmios. Musée Granet, Aix-en-Provence.

rather than a cognate. Not merely is Oghma known as a *trénfher*, 'champion', literally 'strong man', but he is also credited with the invention of the *Ogham* letters, a system of writing based upon the Latin alphabet and consisting of strokes and notches cut upon wood or stone; in its attested form it came into use about the fourth century A.D., but almost certainly it continues an older system of magical symbols.

Much has been written and many theories formulated about Ogmios and Oghma, especially with reference to the enigmatic vignette by Lucian. But all one can say with certainty is, first, that Lucian's Ogmios appears to govern by the power of the spoken

word, and, secondly, that his identification with Hercules – together with the character of the Irish Oghma – marks him out as the divine champion. Beyond this one must risk the errors of speculative interpretation if one is to come closer to the patterns of thought represented for the Celts by Ogmios-Oghma. Perhaps the most interesting and, despite its highly speculative character, the most persuasive of the interpretations so far advanced is that of Françoise Le Roux, which has the considerable merit that it is based on a close analysis of a wide range of early Irish material. According to Mlle Le Roux, Ogmios-Oghma is the god who binds, like the Indian Varuna, a character which manifests itself for example in Lucian's description and in the binding force of the magic *ogham* symbols as used by Cú Chulainn in *Táin Bó Cuailnge* to stay the advance of the Connacht army. She also accepts the older view of Ogmios as a *psychopomp* leading souls from this world to the other. This rests mainly on Lucian's testimony, though one should perhaps add that divinities of death are commonly conceived (like the Indian Yama) as binding gods; in other words, they bind and carry off the dead.

Gaulish 'Dis Pater': Irish Donn

Following his brief commentary on the principal gods of the Gauls, Caesar refers to their belief, as taught by the druids, that they were all descended from Dis Pater. This idea of common descent from a divine ancestor is of course a familiar, one might almost say essential, element of Celtic ideology. It was the normal thing for an Irish tribe to trace its genealogy to an eponymous or other divine ancestor, and some deities like Lugh are the reputed progenitors of many widely scattered peoples. In this light Caesar's remark may be taken merely as a general reference to the ancestor cult. On the other hand it may be significant that he should specifically mention Dis Pater, Roman god of the dead, for it is not unusual that the first man and father of humanity – again the Indian Yama comes to mind

– should also be first of the dead and lord of the underworld. And in point of fact Irish tradition provides a close analogue to the Gaulish Dis Pater.

Donn, 'the brown, or dark, one', is the Irish god of the dead *par excellence*. His abode is a small rocky island, known as *Tech Duinn*, 'the House of Donn', off the south-west coast of Ireland, and he bids his descendants, in other words the people of Ireland, to come to his house when they die (*co tech nDuind frisndálait mairb* 'to the house of Donn where the dead have their tryst'). He is not one of the gods who hold the front of the stage in the early literature and in fact the material concerning him is relatively slight, though quite unambiguous; but his importance, which is implied rather than clearly stated in the early texts, is amply confirmed by the rich variety of the modern folk tradition in which he appears as an imposing and active deity. In the early literary remains he represents on the whole the sombre aspect of the otherworld god as lord of the dead and even tends to be assimilated to the Devil, but the modern tradition, while retaining this underworld characterisation, reveals him in fact as a god of contrasting facets, benign and terrible, creator of storms and shipwrecks and protector of cattle and crops.

It has been argued that, since Donn is revered as the ancestor deity, he is therefore identical with the Daghdha, who is sometimes titled 'the Great Father', with Nuadhu from whom all the Irish were said to be descended, and so on; in other words that he is but one of a number of manifestations of the same great ancestor-deity and lord of the otherworld. Whatever the merits of this argument, its concern is with ultimate origins rather than with the system reflected

Left. Silvanus, lord of the forest and of the hunt, accompanied by his hound. Rheinisches Landesmuseum, Bonn.

Opposite. The god 'Hercules' from High Rochester (Bremenium), Northumberland. Museum of Antiquities, Newcastle upon Tyne.

in the extant sources; for in these, and especially in the earlier of them, Donn is clearly characterised as lord of the dead and is thereby distinguished from the other gods. The very fact that Caesar names 'Dis Pater' as ancestor of the Gauls strongly suggests that this particular role is not an Irish innovation. It explains perhaps why Donn appears in the early literature as a retiring deity, aloof and isolated, who is never found in the society of the other gods. In this respect also he would seem to match the Gaulish 'Dis Pater', who in Caesar's account stands alone and apart from the quintet of main deities. This correspondence serves to vindicate Caesar's account and confirm the ancient autonomy of Donn-Dis Pater.

Sucellus and Nantosvelta

Sucellus, 'the Good Striker' (?), has been identified by some scholars with

'Dis Pater'. He has for companion the goddess *Nantosvelta,* whose name indicates a connection with water (compare the Welsh *nant* meaning 'brook'). His characteristic attribute is his mallet, but he appears also with a cask or a drinking jar and is frequently accompanied by a dog. He is commonly assimilated to *Silvanus,* guardian of forests and patron of agriculture. The mallet and the dog, together with certain other features of his images, have been interpreted as symbols of the underworld deity, while the cask and the drinking jar as also his relationship to Nantosvelta and Silvanus have been taken to symbolise fecundity. There is, of course, no contradiction here, since chthonic deities are often concerned with the fruitfulness of the earth, but it must be admitted that the evidence in the case of Sucellus is not conclusive.

Several other deities in addition to Sucellus have been equated with 'Dis Pater', notably Cernunnos and the Daghdha, and it is true that they have all, in their wide-ranging concern with matters of life and death, certain points of mutual similarity; but in no case do the extant testimonies offer so clear-cut a parallel as in that of Donn and 'Dis Pater'.

Cernunnos

One of the more obvious similarities between insular mythology and Gaulish iconography is their rich profusion of zoomorphic imagery. In sculpture the gods are often accompanied by animals or birds associated with their cult or, in some cases no doubt, with deities conceived in animal form, as in the Paris relief of Esus and the bull. In other instances the animal element actually appears as part of the deity, and of these the most notable is the 'horned god', who bears the horns of stag, ram or bull upon his head. These horn-bearing figures have a long history which extends back far before the emergence of the Celts as a recognisable sociocultural grouping, but in the course of time they apparently became an integral part of the religious thought of the Celtic people.

The earliest example in a clearly Celtic context is that from Val Camonica (see page 49) of about the fourth century B.C. This anticipates a combination of features – antlers, torc and horned serpent – which becomes familiar in the art of a later period, and which takes its common title from a defective instance on a Paris relief found near that of Esus. The lower half of this stone has been broken away, but what remains shows a god with antlers, on each of which hangs a torc, and with cervine as well as human ears. What lends it its peculiar importance, however, is the fact that it alone preserves the name of the god in question, [C]*ernunnos,* 'The Horned (or Peaked) One'. By a convenient licence this name has come to be applied to all images conforming to the type, though naturally it is understood that the deity or deities concerned may have been known by a variety of titles. The Cernunnos type then, as confirmed by other monuments, is of an antlered god, seated in cross-legged fashion, wearing a torc and accompanied by a ram-headed or ram-horned serpent and, less frequently, by a bull and a stag. The characteristic 'Buddhic' posture of the deity has been explained from the fact that the Gauls, as attested by classical authors, were accustomed to sit upon the ground, but the existence of numerous eastern analogues rather suggests that the motif may have had a common source of dissemination in the Near East.

Right. A scene from one of the outer plates of the Gundestrup cauldron, showing a deity holding a stag in either hand. Nationalmuseet, Copenhagen.

Opposite left. The god with the mallet in Roman style. This is the deity who is sometimes named Sucellus, 'The Good Striker'. Musée Lapidaire, Avignon.

Opposite right. The god Sucellus partnered by the goddess Nantosvelta on a relief from Sarreburg, Germany. Sucellus holds his mallet and Nantosvelta her 'dovecot' attribute mounted upon a staff. Underneath in large relief stands a raven which elsewhere accompanies Nantosvelta. Musée de Metz.

Right. Bronze statue of the god with the mallet, from Prémeaux. Musée des Beaux-Arts, Beaune.

Opposite above. The relief of Cernunnos which bears the deity's name. Musée de Cluny, Paris.

Opposite below left. It has long since been remarked that there is a striking analogy between Cernunnos 'lord of the animals' on the Gundestrup cauldron and the Indian god who appears on this seal from Mohenjodaro. Like Cernunnos he is horned, sits cross-legged, and is flanked by various animals. It has been suggested that he is a prototype of the god Shiva in his aspect as Pashupati, 'Lord of Beasts'.

Opposite below right. Horned head from Chesters, Northumberland. Museum of Antiquities, Newcastle upon Tyne.

On the Gundestrup cauldron Cernunnos appears as 'lord of the animals'. In his left hand he holds the ram-headed serpent, on his right stands a magnificent stag, while various other animals are scattered on the surrounding surface. A stela at Reims shows him holding a sack from which a stream of coins pours down towards a bull and a stag standing below: a clear symbol of material prosperity which is corroborated by related monuments. This must refer to Cernunnos's connection with fertility, which is already marked in the Val Camonica carving and is probably implicit in his zoomorphic attributes and his special animal companions. The most constant of these, apart from the stag itself, is the ram-headed serpent which has strong chthonic associations and symbolises fertility.

That the horned god was no stranger to the insular Celts, of the Christian as well as the pre-Christian period, is evidenced by iconographic items from Ireland and Scotland, and one might therefore reasonably have expected to find him in the literary tradition also. There may indeed be an echo of his name in that of Conall *Cernach*, one of the leading heroes of the Ulstermen, and recently on the basis of this postulated relationship Anne Ross has proposed an ingenious and persuasive justification of what

appears to be a rather pointless incident in the Old Irish tale *Táin Bó Fraích*, 'The Driving of Fraích's Cattle'. Conall travels overseas to attack a fortress guarded by a terrible serpent, but in the event the serpent leaps tamely into Conall's girdle and, to quote the text, 'neither did harm to the other'. This strange anticlimax Dr Ross explains by referring it to the statues of Cernunnos from Sommerécourt and Autun, which show the god feeding ram-headed serpents which encircle his waist.

The insular literatures also preserve very many instances of the great herdsman-god analogous to Cernunnos in his role of ruler and protector of the animal kingdom. One of the most striking of these is the monstrous but benign keeper of the forest in the Welsh tale *Owain*. He summoned all the animals, serpents included, through the belling of a stag, and they did obeisance to him 'as humble subjects would do to their lord'. He may even have passed into the *Lives* of the saints, as part of the incalculable debt which Irish hagiography owes to native saga and myth. The sense of close rapport with nature is constant in the *Lives* of the early ascetics – and, incidentally, inspired some of the finest lyric poetry to be found anywhere in pre-modern literature. These holy anchorites lived in intimate communion with animate nature while exercising a paternal

authority over it, and numerous indeed are the instances in their *Lives* of wild animals rendering them homage 'as humble subjects would do to their lord'. It is of course a historical fact that the early saints sought out solitary places and lived close to nature, but in these passages from the *Lives* Christian practice seems to be blended with pre-Christian tradition. A good instance is the account of how St Ciarán of Saighir went into the wilderness and set up a tiny cell, the beginning of his monastery:

'When he came there the holy Ciarán sat down under a tree in the shade of which was a savage-looking boar. On thus seeing a man for the first time the boar fled in terror, but then, being rendered gentle by God, it returned as a servant to the man of God; and that boar was Ciarán's first disciple and, as it were, his first monk in that place. For immediately in view of the man of God it began vigorously to sever branches and grasses with its teeth as materials for the building of a cell. For there was no one else there with the holy man of God, since he had fled alone from his own disciples to that wilderness. Then came other animals from their lairs in the waste to the holy Ciarán: a fox, a badger, a wolf and a stag. And they remained with him in complete submissiveness; for they obeyed the command of the holy man in all things as if they were monks.'

When we read thus of Ciarán's 'community', or of the stag which allowed St Cainnech to use its antlers as a book rest, we see as it were the old mythology taken over and transmuted by the wit and humanity of the scholar-anchorite.

If, however, as Anne Ross has argued cogently, a cult of horned deities of the Cernunnos type once existed among the insular Celts, then one cannot be sure that it petered out in such idyllic innocence. The deity's evident concern with fecundity may have influenced the form of his cult and the content of his myth, and this in turn may explain why artists of the early Christian period tended to assimilate him to Satan and why only residual elements of his myth survive.

In such circumstances the Cernunnos cult would probably have survived longest among the lower orders of society, where custom died hard and orthodoxy was not easily imposed. Unfortunately, this is virtually unknown territory, for it is only in recent times that the usages and beliefs of the common people received conscious recognition in written literature. But if in fact the Cernunnos cult did not quickly wither under the pressure of Christianity, then it is not improbable that traces of it survived into recent times in certain areas of popular custom. But that is another story.

Triadic Groups

The concept of threeness is a more or less universal feature of traditional thought. Among the Indo-Europeans society itself rested upon a threefold classification, as has been demonstrated by Dumézil, and this no doubt impressed the concept still more deeply upon the consciousness of the various peoples of the Indo-

European family. It received particularly free and elaborate expression among the Celts.

In Ireland and Wales the triad was a favourite form for summarising and conserving traditional learning and considerable collections of triadic aphorisms exist in the literatures of both countries. In Wales it was also used extensively as a convenient device for cataloguing characters and episodes in native literature. But of more immediate interest is the fact that the literature itself shows a marked penchant for groups of three characters, and the significant thing about these groups is that very often they represent the triplication of a single personage. Where they bear the same name, the members of the triad are formally differentiated by epithet or attribute; where their names differ, they share a functional identity. This is, moreover, one of the many instances in which iconography and literary tradition confirm and complement each other. Triads of goddesses like the three Brighids do

Left. 'Cernunnos' as 'lord of the animals' upon one of the inner plates of the Gundestrup cauldron. The deity sits in cross-legged position, is crowned by a splendid pair of antlers and wears a torc about his neck. In his left hand he holds a ram-headed serpent, in his right another torc. Nationalmuseet, Copenhagen.

Below left. Panel from North Cross, Ahenny, Co. Tipperary. To the left a man stands behind a palm tree, while before him various animals mingle and fight. No doubt this Christian monument invites a Christian interpretation, but stylistically at least its arrangement of the animals over the available surface evokes comparison with the 'lord of the animals' scene from the Gundestrup cauldron.

Deirdre's elopement to Scotland with Naoise though she was the betrothed of Conchobhar king of Ulster, and of the fatal attraction that drew them back inevitably towards Conchobhar's cruel vengeance. Apart from Naoise his brothers have no personality; in life they are his constant companions and when he dies they likewise must die.

The underlying significance of such ternary groups can only be surmised. Clearly they held a remarkable fascination for the Celts and they must have embodied a rich and vital symbolism, at least for as long as Celtic religion remained intact. And obviously this symbolism need not have been confined to a single level of cognition. It has been observed that triplication may have an intensifying force and that it may also convey the concept of totality. Both or either of these may have been present in the Celtic usage, but one cannot be confident that they exhaust the cognitive value of the tricephalos or of the single personality realised in triple form.

Goddesses: Divine Consorts, Matres

It has often been observed that in their literature the insular Celts, and particularly the Irish, show a remarkable concern with the physical configuration of the land upon which they live. Every river and lake and well, every plain and hill and mountain has its own name, and each name

invite comparison with the triadic grouping of the *Matres,* and, on the other hand, one can hardly dissociate the frequent images of a three-headed divinity from the common literary motif of three brothers comprised within a single unity. This unity is expressed either in the three brothers' undifferentiated equality or in the utter predominance of one of them. The clearest and most absolute instance of the former is that in which three brothers beget the same child. The most celebrated instance of the latter is the tragic story of Deirdre and the three sons of Uisnech. It tells of

Above. A tricephalic deity upon a vase from Bavay (Nord). Cabinet des Médailles, Bibliothèque Nationale, Paris.

Right. Three mother-goddesses, one holding a child, from Vertillum (Côte d'Or). Musée de Chatillon-sur-Seine.

Opposite. A bronze horse mask of the first century A.D. from Stanwick, Yorkshire. British Museum, London.

evokes its own explanatory legend. These legends constituted a distinct branch of native tradition known as *dinnshenchas*, 'the lore of prominent places', which was an important part of the repertoire of the *fili*, the expert in native learning, and which, not surprisingly, became a staple element of literary creation. By the accretion of centuries a vast corpus of this lore came into being which now constitutes one of the richest sources of Celtic mythological tradition. The *dinnshenchas* is thus a kind of comprehensive topography, a legendary

guide to the Irish landscape, and it is for that reason significant that it assigns a conspicuous, even a dominant, role to the female divinities, for it is these, as avatars, or manifestations, of the earth-goddess, who are primarily associated with the land in all its various aspects: its fertility, its sovereignty, its embodiment of the powers of death as well as of life, and so on. Something of this can be glimpsed in Gaulish sculpture, but it is only in the insular literature that it is revealed in all its rich profusion and vigour, and for that reason it will be more convenient to discuss Celtic goddesses within the insular context.

However, two important features of the Gaulish evidence may be mentioned immediately, even though they recur in the insular tradition. The first is the frequent appearance of a goddess as consort of a male deity. Instances are numerous: Sucellus and Nantosvelta, 'Mercury' and Rosmerta, Borvo (Bormo) and Damona, Bormanus and Bormana, Apollo Grannus and Sirona, Mars Lucetius and Nemetona, Mars Visucius and Visucia, Mars Cicolluis and Litavis, Albius and Damona, Luxovius and

Brixia, and so on. In the Celtic context these may all be reduced to the prototypal coupling of the protecting god of tribe or nation with the mother-goddess, and in the wider context of Indo-European mythology they correspond to Indian pairs such as Vishnu and Lakshmi, in which the goddess embodies the *shakti*, or female energy of the god.

One cannot draw any clear or permanent distinction between these divine consorts and the Gaulish divinities honoured under the title of *Matres*, or *Matronae*. This latter cult, which springs from the common concept of the earth as divine mother, was no doubt partly autochthonous and its roots go deep in the mythological tradition of all the Celtic areas. On the monuments the 'mothers' appear most often in groups of three, but also sometimes in pairs or individually. They carry baskets of fruit,

Opposite above right and right. The anthropophagous monster of Noves (Bouches-du-Rhône), known as the 'Tarasque de Noves', probably of the first century B.C. From its gaping jaws protrudes a human arm complete with bracelet while its forepaws rest upon two bearded, severed heads. The detail (right) shows a head. Musée Calvet, Avignon.

Opposite above left. Bearded deity sitting in 'Buddhic' position, found near Autun (Saône-et-Loire). He wears a long, sleeveless garment, a torc around his neck, and a bracelet on his right wrist. He is tricephalic, having a small head projecting from each side of the main one. Above his forehead he has two holes for the insertion of antlers. He appears to be feeding two ram-headed serpents which encircle his body. Above the food and between the serpents' heads the torc emblem is repeated. Musée des Antiquités Nationales, St Germain-en-Laye.

Opposite below. Relief from Reims showing a bearded Cernunnos seated in 'Buddhic' position. He wears a mantle, a torc about his neck and a bracelet on his right upper arm. The antlers which once emerged from his head have been broken away, but they can be reconstructed from traces left on the upper part of the stela. He holds a large sack, from which round objects, evidently coins, flow copiously. Underneath stand a bull and a stag, animals which are elsewhere connected with the Cernunnos cult, and on the pediment over his head there is a large rat, symbol of his chthonic associations. The deity is here flanked by Mercury and Apollo. Musée Saint-Denis, Reims.

cornucopias, babies and other clear symbols of their connection with earthly and human fecundity. Their role and importance are amply illustrated by the insular literature.

Cult Associations of Inanimate Nature

The religious concept which underlies the professedly antiquarian lore of the *dinnshenchas* is expressed more explicitly in the cult of deities who represent or are in some way specially related to particular physical features of the land. The fruitful earth itself was revered as the divine mother who is present, more or less overtly, in all the Celtic goddesses. There were gods of the clearing or cultivated field *(Ialonus)*, of the rock *(Alisanos)*, of the confluence *(Condatis)*, of the fortified place *(Dunatis)*, and others connected with particular mountains and mountainpeaks. The fertilising waters of rivers were normally deified, for example the Seine *(dea Sequana)*,

Marne *(Matrona)*, Saône *(Souconna)*, and the many rivers whose names (from the stem *dēv-*) mean simply 'Divine'. Sources too had their divinities as in *Aventia* (Avenches), *Vesunna* (Périgeux) and *Divona* (Cahors, Bordeaux).

Equally widespread and, in certain circumstances, even more tenacious was the cult of sacred trees. The druids' association with the oak has not been proven beyond reasonable doubt, but the tree-cult in general is well attested by Gaulish dedications and nomenclature. It is in Irish tradition, however, that it is expressed most clearly and consistently, and there is here even a special term for the sacred tree, *bile*, which is no doubt the same word as occurs in the Gaulish *Biliomagus*, 'The Plain of the Sacred Tree'(?). A number of these great trees are mentioned repeatedly in the literature – the Tree of Tortu (an ash), the Oak of Mughna, the Yew of Ross, the Bough of Dathí (an

Opposite. This early rock carving from Val Camonica in northern Italy portrays an antlered deity reminiscent of Cernunnos. However, in this instance the deity stands erect and not in the usual squatting position. He is dressed in a long garment and has a torc upon his right arm and perhaps another on his left. Beneath his left arm hangs an indistinct form which may well be the horned serpent, attribute of Cernunnos. A smaller figure, obviously phallic and evidently a worshipper, stands before the deity.

Below. A little bronze group from Berne, Switzerland, shows the goddess Artio (compare Irish *art*, 'bear') seated before a huge bear close by a tree. The goddess holds a patera containing fruit, which she appears to be offering to the bear, and beside her a basket of fruit stands upon a low pillar. Bernisches Historisches Museum.

_____

ash), the Ash of Uisnech, etc. – but evidently each tribe, or confederation of tribes, had its own sacred tree which stood on the site where the kings of the tribe were duly inaugurated. No doubt, like the universal

World Tree, or *axis mundi*, the tribal tree was supposed in theory to stand at the centre of the tribal territory and to embody its security and integrity. Not infrequently one reads in the Irish Annals of a raiding force invading hostile territory and felling a sacred tree, and quite evidently this was conceived as a dramatic gesture designed to shame and demoralise the people for whom it was both talisman and *crann bethadh,* 'tree of life'.

Cult Associations of Animate Nature

The climax and finale of the saga *Táin Bó Cuailnge* is the conflict of the two great bulls, the *Finnbhennach*, 'White-horned', and the *Donn*, 'Brown', of Cuailnge. When the outcome seemed in the balance, Cormac son of the king of Ulster struck three blows on the brown bull and upbraided him for his weakness. The Donn gave heed, 'for he had human understanding', and attacked with fresh vigour until finally he brought down his adversary. Then he careered across Ireland in his battle rage, scattering fragments of the mangled Finnbhennach from his horns, thereby occasioning the creation of a series of well known historical placenames. When he reached his home in Cuailnge his great heart 'broke like a nut in his breast', and with his death the saga ends.

In this encounter of the two bulls we seem to have the original nucleus of myth around which the extant narrative of *Táin Bó Cuailnge* has been assembled. These animals are not of this world: they reached their present state, we are told, only after a prolonged series of metamorphoses during which they assumed the form of ravens, stags, champions, water beasts, demons, and water worms, and in the beginning they were the swineherds of two of the lords of the otherworld. Here the shapeshifting which is such a commonplace of Celtic tradition serves to link the anthropomorphic and zoomorphic aspects of the deity, so that the text becomes almost like a gloss on much of the iconography. For these are divine swineherds, avatars of the herdsman-god

who crops up so very frequently in Celtic literature and who has an analogue in the Vedic Pushan, and several in Greek. Thus by one of the myriad involutions which make Celtic mythology both interesting and intractable we are once more close to Cernunnos, lord of the animals.

The Brown Bull of Cuailnge can scarcely be dissociated from the Tarvos Trigaranus, the Three-horned bull, whose images are found both in Gaul and in Britain. And since names of persons, places and populations commonly echo those of deities, one can safely postulate a conceptual relationship between the Donn of Cuailnge and a number of widely attested names which seem to imply familiarity with the notion of a bull-deity. Particularly interesting is the Gaulish name *Donnotaurus*, 'Brown, or Kingly, Bull'. It is evident, then, that the divine bull figured prominently in the mythology of all the Celtic peoples, and *Táin Bó Cuailnge*, greatest of the Irish sagas, is therefore a fitting as well as a lasting monument to his remarkable prestige.

But the bull is only one of a number of animals and birds which had special cult associations for the Celts. Cernunnos was related to the stag, the ram-headed serpent, the bull, and also, in a less immediate sense, to the whole of the animal world. In addition, the iconographic record comprises boars, horses, dogs, bears, etc., as well as fish and various types of birds, all of them connected more or less closely with certain deities. Not surprisingly this diversity is reproduced in the insular tradition, and in such complexity and abundance as to defy any neat classification. Of all these supernatural creatures the boar is probably the most notable. Frequently it is the fierce, destructive quarry who leads its hunters to the otherworld, and generally we are told that it was anthropomorphic until transformed. Its mythological importance is not unconnected with the fact – abundantly attested in archaeology and literature – that the Celts esteemed pork as the choicest of foods both in this world and in the next, and in Irish legend the undiminishing

otherworld food is sometimes represented in the form of a pig which, though killed and cooked each evening, is alive and whole the next morning. The Gaulish Mercury occurs with the epithet *Moccus* (Welsh *moch*, 'pigs') and obviously this refers to a native deity concerned in some capacity with pigs, as hunter perhaps or as divine swineherd.

Supernatural horses are frequent. Sometimes, particularly in folktales, they carry mortals off to the otherworld of the dead, but generally their role was a sympathetic one: it may be recalled that horse-racing was a feature of the great seasonal assemblies and one of the pleasures especially associated with the otherworld. *Epona*, 'The Divine Horse' or 'The Horse Goddess', was one of the more important Gaulish deities, winning

Above. Statuette of the horse-goddess Epona from Alésia. As usual, she is shown riding side-saddle. Musée Alésia, Alise-Sainte-Reine.

Opposite. A stone sculpture of a deity with a boar from Euffigneix, Haute Marne, first century A.D. The torc which the deity wears is a common attribute of divine figures. Musée des Antiquités Nationales, St Germain-en-Laye.

especial favour among the cavalry of the Roman army. She may have an Irish analogue in *Édaín Echraidhe* (*echraidhe*, 'horse-riding'), and some scholars have seen an equivalent of her in the Welsh *Rhiannon*. There was also a *Dea Artio* (as well as a Mercury *Artaios*), obviously connected with the bear (Irish *art*, 'bear'), and a *Dea Arduinna* who is shown seated on a wild bore. With this type one may compare the Irish goddess

Flidhais who ruled over the beasts of the forests and whose cattle were the wild deer.

Magic or divine birds are equally numerous. There are deities who assume bird form occasionally – one of the characteristic Celtic motifs is of swans linked by a silver chain, the symbol of divine beings metamorphosed – and there are those, the war-goddesses, who do so constantly; one of the names given to them is *Badhbh*, 'Raven, Hooded-crow'. There are also the wondrous birds who figure in almost all accounts of the Happy Otherworld and who lull men to sleep with the soothing sweetness of their music; these are assigned to Rhiannon in the *Mabinogi* and probably correspond to the birds who accompany a goddess on a number of sculptures.

It has been suggested that the wealth of animal and bird imagery in Celtic mythology, and particularly the intermingling of animal and human forms in the characterisation of the deities, points to the coexistence of inferior (or primitive) and evolved forms of Celtic divinity. But such a view rests upon the assumption that, at least on the higher level of belief, there was a gradual evolution from a zoomorphic to an anthropomorphic conception of divinity, and for this there is no real evidence. What is clear, however, is that the Celtic idea of the otherworld, as this is realised in the literature, allowed remarkable imaginative fluidity with the natural and supernatural seeming continually to merge and commingle in an almost free variation, and it is perhaps in this light that one should view the regular and easy interchange of zoomorphic and anthropomorphic images.

Opposite. Torso of Mercury of Puy de Jouer at Saint-Goussaud. Musée de Guéret.

Below. Bronze boar with stylised back-bristles from Neuvy-en-Sullias (Loiret), probably first century B.C. Musée Historique, Orléans.

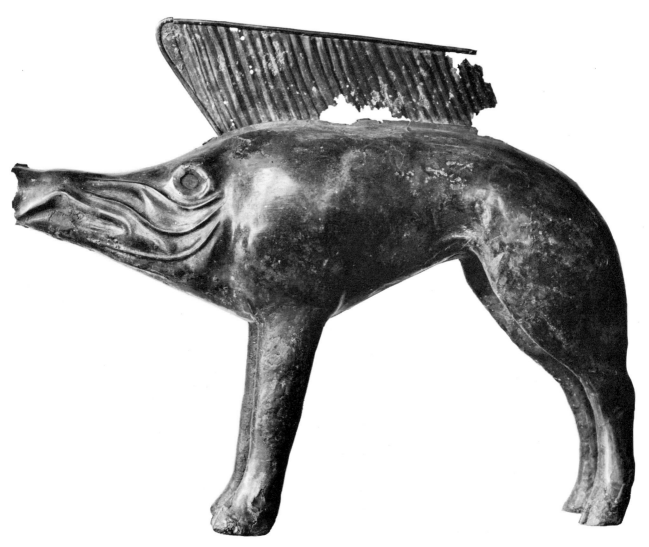

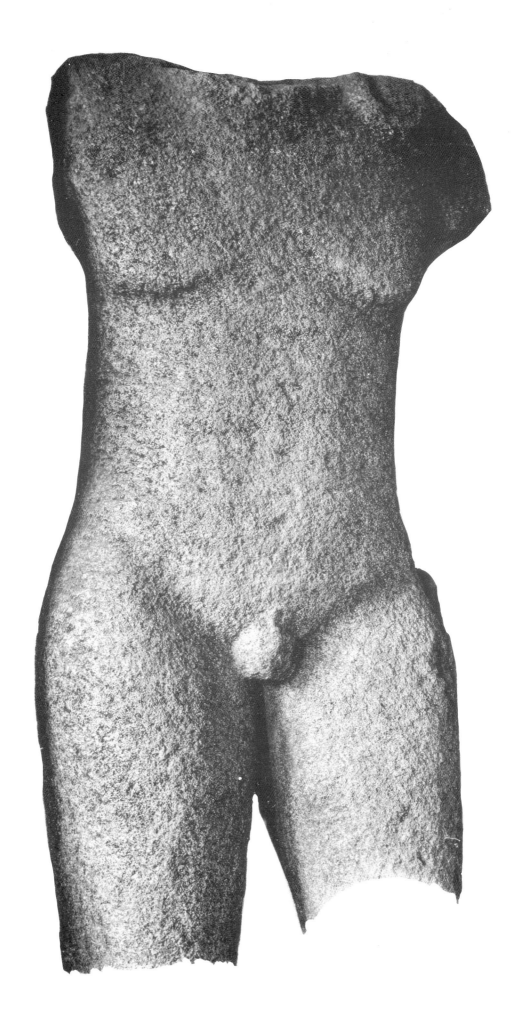

The Tuatha Dé Danann

The Book of Invasions

The Celts have left no native myth of the world's creation, though it would be strange if they lacked one. Caesar speaks of the Gaulish druids' concern with the nature of the material universe as well as with the powers of the gods, and it may be that he had heard of such a cosmogony at second hand. If so, it is to Irish tradition that one would naturally look for the evidence, and unfortunately, though understandably, Irish tradition is here defective. For the monastic scholars who, in the late sixth and the seventh century, set about compiling a record of the Irish people and its origins were no mere amanuenses to native tradition; their guiding purpose was to accommodate this tradition within the framework provided by the Bible and early Christian historians like Eusebius and Orosius, and to this end they doctored it and grafted it on to the Christian account of human origins. Adam became the ancestor of the Irish as of the rest of humanity, though, as we have already seen, Donn was not forgotten.

This re-writing of tradition was progressively elaborated during the following centuries until finally, in the twelfth, it culminated in the pseudo-history entitled *Leabhar Gabhála Éireann,* 'The Book of the Conquest of Ireland', commonly known as the *Book of Invasions*. The 'conquest' of the title refers no doubt to the arrival of the Gaels, but in the extant compilation this is in fact the last of a series of six immigrations. The first of these preceded the Flood and was led by Cesair, who was a daughter of Bith son of Noah, or alternatively by Banbha, one of the eponyms of Ireland. All perished in the Flood except Fintan, who survived through many ages and through the successive invasions in the form of a salmon, an eagle and a hawk and was consequently invoked as a witness to the events of the Irish past. Next came Partholón and his followers. He fought a battle against a race of demonic beings known as Fomhoire, and this was the first battle fought in Ireland. He cleared four plains – hitherto there had been only one in Ireland – and during his time seven lakes appeared. He also instituted many crafts and customs for the first time: the first guesting-house was built, the first beer and ale brewed, legal suretyship was established for the first time, and so on. Finally he and his people were wiped out by a plague.

The third invasion was led by Nemhedh. Four lakes were formed in his time and twelve plains were cleared. It is evident that this and the preceding invasions were conceived of as imparting to the land of Ireland its geographical definition and identity. By creating its physical features and assigning names to them they may be said, in a mythological sense, to have brought it into existence. However much of the detail of these invasions may be late invention, this conception at least seems old.

After Nemhedh's death his people lived under the sway of the Fomhoire, and each year on the feast of Samhain, the first of November, they had to pay a tribute of two-thirds of their corn, their milk and their children. At last in desperation they rose against their masters and attacked their island stronghold, but only one boat's complement of thirty men survived the battle and of these one section went to 'Greece' and another to the 'north of the world'. It is from these remnants of Nemhedh's people that

Right. Bronze handle mount in the form of a stylised owl's head from a large cauldron, the remains of which were found in a bog at Brå, Jutland; third century B.C. The cauldron was deliberately smashed and may have been a religious offering. The custom of perching animal heads on the rim of cauldrons to oversee the contents comes ultimately from the East but was adopted by Celtic craftsmen, particularly in central Europe where this cauldron was probably manufactured. Forhistorisk Museum, Moesgaard.

Below. Two playfully pugnacious little bronze bulls with legs spread and tails upraised (and each ending in a kind of rosette) which may have been mountings from a chariot yoke. They were discovered in a earth-work at Bulbury Camp in Dorset and probably belong to the first century A.D. Dorset County Museum, Dorchester.

the next two settlements of Ireland supposedly derive. Those of them who went to 'Greece' multiplied and eventually returned to Ireland, where they constituted the peoples known as the Fir Bholg, the Gailioin, and the Fir Dhomhnann. There is no longer any mention of lakes being formed or

plains cleared; the historical land of Ireland is already a reality, and, appropriately, the main innovations credited to the Fir Bholg are socio-political in character. They divided the country into five, thereby instituting the provinces (Irish *cóigedh*, 'a province', literally 'a fifth'); these comprise Ulster, Leinster, Munster and Connacht, representing the four cardinal points, together with Meath, which consisted of an area around the centre of the country at Uisnech. This division, as the brothers Rees have pointed out, reproduces a fivefold conception of the world which is more or less universal and is particularly well attested in India and China. The Fir Bholg also introduced kingship and the notion of its sacred character. One of their kings, Eochaidh mac Eirc, was the prototype of the just ruler: 'No rain fell during his reign, but only the dew; there was no year without harvest. Falsehood was banished from Ireland during his

Above. Trapezoid bronze plaque from Tal y Llyn, Merionethshire, first century B.C. to first century A.D. The complete plaque, or what remains intact, bears two opposed heads linked by a common neck. National Museum of Wales, Cardiff.

Opposite left. Ogham stone from Kilmalkedar, Co. Kerry. The Ogham characters can be seen on the vertical edges of the stone. Over 300 of these monuments survive in Ireland, mostly in the southern counties. There are 57 in Britain, 40 of them in Wales, and virtually all of them in areas settled by the Irish in early times.

Opposite right. Stone figure with janiform head and leafcrown from Holzgerlingen, Württemberg (see also pages 7 and 63). Württembergisches Landesmuseum, Stuttgart.

time, and he it was who first established the rule of justice there.' Thus is created the rapport – fundamental to the concept of sacral kingship – that exists between the righteousness of the ruler and the prosperity of his

kingdom. Equally indicative of the new order with its warrior aristocracy is the fact that Eochaidh was the first king to be slain by a weapon.

In view of this role assigned to the Fir Bholg in the creation of the classical Irish social system, it is perhaps significant that they are the first of the *Leabhar Gabhála* settlers with a foot – albeit a rather unsteady one – in history. The Gailioin are identified with the Laighin, who gave their name to the province of Leinster, and the Fir Dhomhnann (or Domhnainn), who are attested mainly in Connacht, are no doubt related to the Dumnonii of Britain. It seems clear that at this stage history and mythology coalesce within the framework of the ancient invasion legend.

The next invaders were the Tuatha Dé Danann, 'The People of the Goddess Danu', who had become skilled in the arts of druidry and magic during their sojourn in the northern islands of the world. They brought

with them four talismans: the stone of Fál which shrieked under a lawful king; the spear of Lugh which ensured victory; the sword of Nuadha from which none could escape; and the cauldron of the Daghdha from which none would go unsatisfied. On their arrival they demanded battle or the kingship from the Fir Bholg, and from this ensued the First Battle of Magh Tuiredh in which the Fir Bholg were defeated. But the Tuatha Dé did not enjoy their supremacy for long unchallenged: soon they were compelled to do battle with the ancient adversary, the Fomhoire.

The Second Battle of Magh Tuiredh

As well as the references in *Leabhar Gabhála* there is an independent epic account of this battle which constitutes one of the most important sources of Irish mythology. The origins of the conflict and its development are there recorded.

During the First Battle of Magh Tuiredh, that in which the Fir Bholg were defeated, Nuadha king of the Tuatha Dé lost an arm, and since physical defects were incompatible with the ancient concept of kingship, it was necessary that he should be replaced. The choice fell – rather oddly it might seem at first glance – on *Bres*, 'the Beautiful', whose father Elatha was a king of the Fomhoire, but who was reared among the Tuatha Dé, his mother's kin. Soon

however Bres's rule became oppressive and the country fell in thrall to the kings of the Fomhoire. The Daghdha was reduced to digging and building a fort for Bres and Oghma to fetching firewood. Moreover, Bres lacked what is the mark of every true king: generosity. The chiefs of the Tuatha Dé complained that 'their knives were not greased by him, and however often they visited him their breaths did not smell of ale.' There was no entertainment for them in the royal household, no poets, musicians, acrobats or buffoons. In the end retribution was hastened – as so often afterwards in Irish tradition – by a poet's verses. When Coirbre the poet of the Tuatha Dé was received by Bres with scant hospitality, he retaliated with a magic-tipped satire – the first that was made in Ireland – 'and nought save decay was on Bres from that hour'. The leaders of the Tuatha Dé demanded that he should renounce the kingship and he then set out to muster an army of the Fomhoire in his support.

In the meantime Nuadha had been fitted by Dian Cécht the leech with an arm of silver and was reinstated in the sovereignty, and from that time forth he was known as Nuadha Airgedlámh, 'Nuadha of the Silver Hand, Arm'. Then follows the episode of Lugh's arrival and his admission to the royal court (see page 25), and this is the prelude to a curious exchange of roles: no sooner had Nuadha proof of Lugh's polytechnic competence than he relinquished the royal seat to him in the hope that he would lead the Tuatha Dé to victory against the Fomhoire. Under Lugh's direction preparations are set on foot and each of the craftsmen and the magicians of the Tuatha Dé promises his own special contribution: the craftsman to fashion wondrous weapons, the sorcerer to hurl the mountains of Ireland on the Fomhoire, the cupbearer to conceal from them the waters of Ireland's lakes and rivers, the druid to cast upon them three showers of fire, to deprive them of two-thirds of their strength and valour and to bind in their bodies the urine of humans and horses.

Once the battle was joined, the slaughter was great on both sides. But whereas the slain of the Fomhoire remained so, those of the Tuatha Dé were cast into a well over which Dian Cécht and his three children sang spells, and by its magic efficacy they were restored to life. Lugh also had recourse to his magic powers: moving around the men of his army 'on one foot and with one eye' he chanted an incantation to lend them strength and courage. He thus assumed a characteristic posture of the sorcerer and one which reproduced the monstrous form ascribed by tradition to the Fomhoire. He then faced the dreaded Balar 'of the baleful eye'. Balar's eye was such that it required four men to raise its lid, and when uncovered its venomous gaze could disable an army. But as soon as Lugh saw the eye open against him he cast a sling-stone which drove it through to the back of Balar's head so that it wrought destruction on his own followers. The Fomhoire were routed and expelled for ever from Ireland. Bres himself was captured and sought to save his life by promising, first that the cattle of Ireland should always be in milk, and secondly, that there should be a harvest in every quarter of the year. Both offers were rejected, but he was finally spared in return for advice as to the proper times for ploughing, sowing and reaping.

This is in substance the story of the Second Battle of Magh Tuiredh. Its mythological importance is obvious, its meaning rather less so. It has been argued by T. F. O'Rahilly that the essential part of the tale is a myth of the slaying of Balar by Lugh and that the rest has been assembled artificially around this nucleus, and his argument is buttressed by the fact that such an opposition between an elder established deity and a younger and versatile rival was evidently a familiar one to Irish tradition. On the other hand, it is questionable whether the extant narrative of the Battle of Magh Tuiredh can be plausibly reduced to this elemental theme, and it may legitimately be objected that O'Rahilly has taken no account of comparable traditions of theomachy from within the Indo-European field that had long since been referred to by earlier scholars. For example an analogy has been drawn more than once between the Tuatha Dé and the Fomhoire on the one hand and the Devas and the Asuras of India on the other. In both these instances the demonic powers wage a continual struggle against the gods and the cosmic order which they command, though in Irish tradition as recorded this contest has been given a historical cast and has become securely localised on Irish soil. In more recent times the problem of the Second Battle of Magh Tuiredh has inserted itself discreetly but quite firmly within the framework of Professor Georges Dumézil's

Opposite. Dún Aonghusa on Inishmore, biggest of the Aran Islands. This massive stone fort dates from the Iron Age, probably from the last half of the first millennium B.C., and it is one of the finest examples of its type. Tradition has it that it was built by the Fir Bholg, who were expelled from the mainland of Ireland.

Below and right. Two bronze wine-flagons of the fourth century B.C., from Basse-Yutz (Moselle). They are a pair and show only minor discrepancies. The little duck on the spout is evidently quite unaware that it is menaced by the two animals on the lid and the larger animal which forms the handle. Right is the zoomorphic handle of one of the flagons. The ring of the lid-chain passes through the tongue and lower jaw. In the middle of the handle is a double palmette once filled with enamel, and the base of the handle is formed by a bearded mask with coral eyes. British Museum, London.

structuralist comparative studies of Indo-European mythology, and this has led to certain penetrating and plausible suggestions regarding the inner meaning of the tale.

The kernel of Dumézil's ideas on Indo-European mythology is his theory of the 'three functions'. These, he claims, are the basis of a tripartite classification which manifests itself both in mythology and in social organisation. The first function concerns the administration of the universe and has two aspects, the one magico-religious, the other rational and juridical. In the Indian context it is embodied in the *Brahman* caste and its two aspects are assigned to the gods Varuna and Mitra respectively. The second consists in the exercise of physical force, 'primarily but not solely of a warlike nature'. It is embodied in the *Kshatriya* or warrior caste and its divine personification is

the god Indra. The third comprises all the manifestations of the notion of fertility: prosperity, health, fecundity in plant and animal life, peace, voluptuousness and numerical weight. It is embodied in the *Vaishya* or farmer caste and is promoted by a number of deities of whom the most prominent are the Ashvins. But this inner system, Dumézil argues, is not merely Indian or Indo-Iranian, but Indo-European, and his constant endeavour has been to demonstrate its reality within the different societies and traditions of the Indo-European family. And even though his researches have not been uniformly successful in this regard, the cumulative weight of the evidence shows beyond reasonable doubt that the formal recognition of some kind of tripartite classification based on functional differentiation is an inherent characteristic of the Indo-European heritage.

Among the Celts the stratification of Indian society is closely paralleled by the early Irish classification of druids, warrior nobles *(flatha)* and freemen *(bó-airigh)*, which in turn corresponds to Caesar's division of Gaulish society into *druides, equites* and *plebs.* On the other hand, the tripartite division of the Indian pantheon is not obviously paralleled among the Irish deities, though it should be pointed out that the extant record of the early Irish social system is undoubtedly more authentic and unadulterated than that of the Irish gods and their spheres of activity. Even as the tradition stands, the Irish deities do not lack definable functions, but that these constitute, or formerly constituted, a hierarchy of three distinct levels awaits clear demonstration.

In point of fact, however, for the purpose of Dumézil's views on the Tuatha Dé and the Second Battle of Magh Tuiredh it is only necessary that he should demonstrate a real distinction between the deities of the third function and the rest. For in a number of separate studies he has argued persuasively that within the tripartite system there is an inherent dualism which tends to unite the two higher functions in opposition to the third. This dualism gave rise to a myth which may be traced in several branches of Indo-European tradition and which recounts how the gods of the lowest function were admitted to the community of the higher gods only after a struggle in which each side had threatened to destroy the other. He instances the Scandinavian tradition of the war of the Aesir and the Vanir and their subsequent reconciliation: the Aesir combine the gods of the first function (represented by Odin) and the second (Thor), while the Vanir embody the third (Njord, Freyr and Freyja). Similarly, he claims that the Second Battle of Magh Tuiredh is but another reflex of the Indo-European myth. The Tuatha Dé, when they arrived in Ireland, did not command all the competences necessary to a settled society. In the persons of their leaders they had at their disposal druidic magic

(the Daghdha), warrior prowess (Oghma), the totality of arts and crafts (Lugh), and the important techniques of medicine and smith-work (Dian Cécht and Goibhniu), but they completely lacked the third function in its most necessary form: agriculture. On the contrary, it fell to their opponents, the Fomhoire, to supply this lack, and this is epitomised in the agreement by which Bres is granted his life in return for the secrets of agricultural prosperity.

This interpretation leaves certain loose ends which have not gone unnoticed by Dumézil. In the first place, the battle ends in the total subjection of the Fomhoire, not in a reconciliation and fusion with the Tuatha Dé, as the proto-myth would imply, and secondly, the Fomhoire are consistently pictured elsewhere in Irish tradition as demons, not as gods (their name means literally 'under-demons', that is to say, inferior or perhaps undersea demons). The answer proposed is that these inconsistencies with the postulated proto-myth are in fact secondary and derive from their actual context. When the battle of the gods was included within the pseudo-history of the invasions and its primary significance obscured, the opponents of the Tuatha Dé were confused with the Fomhoire, the traditional enemies of cosmic order, and this in turn entailed a change in the outcome of the struggle. In favour of this line of argument one may adduce the fact that the Fomhoire of the Second Battle of Magh Tuiredh have personal links with the Tuatha Dé and are described in terms which are more appropriate to the latter than to the monstrous Fomhoire of other texts. For this in itself strongly suggests that the opponents of the Tuatha Dé in this particular battle were themselves gods.

Dumézil's interpretation of the Second Battle of Magh Tuiredh is not beyond controversy, but nevertheless it is highly plausible and has the not inconsiderable merit of recovering order and purpose from apparent chaos. Apart from its central thesis, it argues the existence of a coherent system of gods inherited from the Indo-European past – which has sometimes been disputed – and in this lies much of its importance for the study of Irish, and Celtic, mythology.

The Coming of the Gaels

In the scheme of *Leabhar Gabhála* all that has preceded is merely by way of leading up to the advent of the Sons of Míl, whose descendants, the Gaels, were henceforth to be the dominant people of Ireland. The scholastic provenance of the account of this invasion is obvious: the Sons of Míl come to Ireland from Spain because it was believed that *Hibernia*, the Latin name for Ireland, was derived from *Iberia*, while their father's name Míl Espáine is simply the Latin *miles*

Hispaniae, 'soldier of Spain', in Irish dress. But, despite its transparent fabrications, there is much in this account that is evidently traditional.

The Sons of Míl landed in the south-west of Ireland on the feast of Beltene (1 May) and, as the poet Amhairghin set his right foot upon Irish soil, he sang this poem in which, like Vishnu's avatar Krishna in the *Bhagavad-Gita*, he claims to subsume all being within himself:

I am an estuary into the sea.
I am a wave of the ocean.
I am the sound of the sea.
I am a powerful ox.
I am a hawk on a cliff.
I am a dewdrop in the sun.
I am a plant of beauty.
I am a boar for valour.
I am a salmon in a pool.
I am a lake in a plain.
I am the strength of art . . .

Having defeated the Tuatha Dé Danann, the Sons of Míl set out towards Tara. On their way they encountered the three divine eponyms of Ireland, *Banbha*, *Fódla*, and *Ériu*, and each of the three won from them a promise that the island would bear her name. To Amhairghin the *fili*, who assured her that hers would be its principal name, Ériu foretold that Ireland would belong to the Sons of Míl for all time, but to Donn, their chief, who addressed her with scant courtesy, she announced that neither he nor his children would have benefit of the island. In the event, he was drowned off the south-west coast and buried on the island known ever since as *Tech nDuinn* 'The House of Donn'. At Tara the Sons of Míl found the three kings of the Tuatha Dé, Mac Cuill, Mac Cécht and Mac Gréine, husbands of the three goddesses, and called upon them to surrender the

land, but instead the kings claimed a respite and referred its conditions to the judgement of Amhairghin. The poet's decision was that the Sons of Míl should re-embark and retire beyond the ninth wave (which for the Celts constituted a magic boundary). But when they sought to land again, the Tuatha Dé created a 'druidic' wind which carried them out to sea. Then Amhairghin arose and addressed himself directly to the land of Ireland ('I invoke the land of Ireland . . .'), and immediately the wind abated and the sea was calmed. The Sons of Míl came ashore and inflicted a final defeat on the Tuatha Dé at Tailtiu, site of the annual festival instituted by Lugh.

As yet, one cannot say with any assurance just how much of this account is pseudo-historical invention; it is easier to say what is not. Amhairghin, like Donn, is wholly

mythological, and it is noteworthy that it is he who, as seer and arbiter, takes precedence of all the rest of the Sons of Míl. It is he who ensures their landing by appeasing the divinity of Ireland and who symbolises the beginnings of their settlement by proclaiming himself the embodiment of all creation. And in his invocation of Ireland as in the triad of eponymous goddesses married to the kings of Tara we find eloquent expression of one of the dominant themes of Irish tradition: the personification of the land as a goddess who is joined in marriage to her rightful king.

The Retreat of the Tuatha Dé

Despite their defeat, the Tuatha Dé still retained the power of their magic arts and they deprived the Gaels of their corn and milk until they forced them to come to terms. It was then decided that the country should be divided into two parts, the lower half going to the Tuatha Dé and the upper half to the Gaels. Thus the Tuatha Dé retired underground and the Daghdha assigned to each of their chiefs a *sídh* or 'fairy mound', and throughout the countryside such mounds are still regarded – or were until very recently – as the special dwelling places of the fairy people. Already in the late seventh century a clerical biographer of St Patrick refers to the 'sídh or gods who dwell in the earth' *(side aut deorum terrenorum)*, thus evidently taking for granted the tradition that placed the native gods under the earth's surface.

This *modus vivendi* serves to explain how the Tuatha Dé came to be securely established in the Irish landscape, living in close proximity to its human inhabitants who are ever and always conscious of their presence. Theirs is the other, the hidden face of

Above. This sandstone head from Heidelberg, of fifth to fourth century B.C., probably belonged to a pillar statue such as those from Pfalzfeld (see page 7) and Holzgerlingen (see page 56). Like other such heads it is a Janus, but in this instance the face on the reverse side is reduced to a few curved lines; of 'this counterpoint between the explicit and the illusory', J. V. S. Megaw remarks that it 'is typical Celtic visual punning'. It has two motifs which are a feature of this phase of La Tène art (compare the Pfalzfeld stone): the two lobes which surmount the head – sometimes referred to as a 'leaf-crown' – and the trefoil pattern on the forehead. Both symbols seem to be indicative of the sacred and the supernatural. Badisches Landesmuseum, Karlsruhe.

Opposite. Silver-coated torc from Trichtingen, Württemberg. It is over 13 pounds (6 kg) in weight and was probably a votive object. The torc was not merely an article of personal ornament among the Celts, but also had a positive, though ill-defined, socio-religious significance and often appears on images of the gods. Württembergisches Landesmuseum, Stuttgart.

Ireland and it tends increasingly to reflect the features of the visible one. They have their local and provincial kings and their whole social organisation resembles that of the human community. They have the same local loyalties, the same internal dissensions and petty warfare, and indeed, as this suggests, their divinity does not render them permanently invulnerable nor exempt from violent death. Yet, paradoxically, the quality that most clearly sets them apart is their immortality, by virtue of which they live 'without grief, without sorrow, without death . . . without age, without corruption of the earth'. If there is a contradiction here it is not one which demands to be resolved by rational argument. One of the characteristics of the otherworld with which Irish and Welsh imagination makes constant play is the relativity of time and space: perspectives are reversed and brevity becomes length and length brevity as one crosses the tenuous border between the natural and the supernatural. No doubt the violent deaths of some of the Tuatha Dé should be viewed in a similar light. At all events, it is clear that in this mythic environment where opposites combine and interchange, the Irish storyteller saw nothing amiss in the occasional mortality of the immortal gods.

The other feature which conspicuously distinguishes the lords of the *sídh* from mortal kings and heroes is their control of magic, and it is this rather than the notion of divinity which characterises their role in most of the early literature. In this respect the early literary tale and the modern folk tale are at one. Theirs is an idealised, magic counterpart of the natural world into which mortals rarely intrude except by invitation or by accident. Conversely, the people of the *sídh* do not normally intervene in human affairs, and the idea that humans should invoke them as deities is almost entirely absent. But it would be unwise to assume too readily that this was always so. There are at least two considerations to be kept in mind. In the first place, while the attitude of the monastic redactors to the traditions of native paganism was a remarkably liberal one, it nevertheless preserved its own order of emphasis and there were certain matters on which it allowed little compromise: supplication and adoration of the native deities would have been one of these. An eighth-century hymn declares that until St Patrick preached the Gospel the Irish people adored the gods of the *sídh:* St Patrick knew his priorities and so, presumably, did the clerical *literati* of later centuries. The second consideration is more obvious, but no less important. We know that the Celts were not the first people to settle in Ireland, and it would be unrealistic to suppose that the traditions and beliefs of the indigenous population were annulled by their arrival. There is in fact a strong presumption that the literary account is coloured by this popular substratum which came into its own once more as the Celtic gods were depreciated through the establishment of Christianity and the influence of its teaching.

The Daghdha

Of the leaders of the Tuatha Dé only two remain to be discussed, the *Daghdha* and *Nuadha*. The Daghdha, literally the 'Good God', was their doyen and king and was known also as *Eochaidh Ollathair,* 'Eochaidh the Great Father'. He was credited with much wisdom, and another of his names or titles describes him as the *Ruadh Rofhessa,* 'The Mighty One of Great Knowledge'. It is fitting therefore that he should also be qualified, as he is on several occasions, as a god of druidism.

He has two special attributes, his club and his cauldron. The latter is the characteristic vessel of plenty of the Celtic otherworld 'from which no company ever went unsatisfied'. Its possession identifies him as lord of the otherworld and its eternal abundance, and it was no doubt in this capacity that he was reputed 'to control the weather and the crops'. His marvellous club was such that one end killed the living and the other revived the dead, and when he dragged it behind him, it left a track as deep as the boundary ditch between two provinces. It corresponds to Thor's hammer and the *vajra* or 'thunderbolt' of Indra, and it also suggests a comparison between the Daghdha and the Gaulish *Sucellos*, 'The Good Striker'(?). In battle it strewed the bones of the enemy upon the ground 'as numerous as hailstones under the hooves of horses'.

The Daghdha provides a striking instance of the ancient tendency to treat gods and father-figures as objects of fun and ridicule. Though short garments were the mark of the churl and the vagabond entertainer, the Daghdha's tunic barely reached as far as his rump. And if his dress was uncouth, his behaviour at times was even more so. Before the Second Battle of Magh Tuiredh he was sent by Lugh to spy out the enemy position and to delay the engagement. The Fomhoire granted him a truce and prepared for him a prodigious porridge – 'and this was done to mock him, for he had a great weakness for porridge'. They filled the king's cauldron with eighty measures of milk and the same of meal and fat, and to this they added goats and sheep and swine. When the contents were boiled, they were poured into a hole in the ground – an effective caricature of the cauldron of abundance

Right. A hunter god from La Celle-Mont-Saint-Jean (Sarthe). He carries a bow and a billhook and the remains of horns are seen on his head. Musée des Antiquités Nationales, St Germain-en-Laye.

Opposite. Wrought-iron mask, presumably of a Gaulish deity, from Alençon (Maine-et-Loire). Musée St Jean, Angers.

– and the Daghdha was ordered to eat the lot or be slain. So he took up his ladle, 'which was so big that a man and woman could have lain together in it', and began to eat; and when he was finished, he scraped the gravelly bottom of the hole with his finger and then dozed off to sleep. There follows a humourously grotesque account of his love-making with the daughter of one of the Fomhoire, as a result of which she promises to turn her magic against her own people. This parallels an earlier episode in which the Daghdha goes to tryst with a woman on the feast of *Samhain* (1 November). He finds her standing astride the river Unius in Connacht, washing, and has intercourse with her, and she promises her assistance in the coming battle. The text identifies her as the *Morríghan*, the goddess of war, but in any event it is already clear from the circumstance in which the Daghdha finds her that she is in fact the war fury, here in the familiar guise of the dread female who is seen before a battle washing the mangled heads and limbs of those who are destined to die.

These incidents are a testimony – perhaps an unconscious one on the part of the redactor – to the status of the Daghdha; paradoxical as it may appear, it is by virtue of his seniority that he is made a figure of fun. In the eating episode there is obvious comedy in his making a pleasure, if not a virtue, of necessity, and this the redactor has pointed up neatly, but in the light of the evidence for ritual over-eating in other parts of the world it can hardly be doubted that

the Daghdha's voracity derives from myth and not from some monastic storyteller's fertile imagination. His tryst with the Morríghan is still more significant. She is the goddess of slaughter who prefigures and in certain measure decides the outcome of battle, and by his physical union with her he ensures victory and security for his people. Nothing could more clearly underline his role of father-figure among the gods.

Irish Nuadha: Welsh Nudd

Nuadha Airgedlámh, 'Nuadha of the Silver Hand, or Arm', has a namesake in Welsh. The tale of *Culhwch and Olwen* mentions a *Lludd Llaw Ereint* whose name evidently derives by alliterative assimilation from *Nudd Llaw Ereint*, the exact counterpart of the Irish *Nuadha Airgedlámh*. Almost nothing is known of him under this name, but he can hardly be dissociated from the Lludd son of Beli who is the hero of the Middle Welsh tale *Lludd and Llefelys*. The original Welsh equivalent of *Nuadha*, viz. *Nudd*, also crops up in mythological contexts, but its related traditions have almost completely perished. Its former importance in British tradition has, however, been confirmed by the discovery at Lydney Park in Gloucestershire of the remains of a Romano-British temple containing dedications to a god *Nodons* (or *Nodens*), whose name corresponds etymologically to Nuadha and Nudd.

The obvious syncretism of the Lydney Park cult makes it difficult to assess the significance of the objects found there. Thus some of them would suggest that the god had strong aquatic associations, and yet these are not noticeably reflected in the legends of Nuadha and his Welsh congeners. What we know for certain of this insular god can therefore be summed up very briefly. According to the Irish evidence Nuadha was a king of Ireland who relinquished his sacred office twice, first when he suffered a physical blemish and secondly when he stood down so that the hero-figure Lugh might defend the country against a race of invaders. In the Welsh tale of *Lludd and Llefelys*

Lludd was the king of Britain who sought the advice of his brother Llefelys in order to rid the kingdom of three oppressions, and one of these was an invasion by a magic people known as Coraniaid. One may discern a possible parallel here, allowing for divergent evolution of the two literatures: Nuadha and Lludd find their respective kingdoms threatened from outside and win relief through the aid of Lugh and Llefelys. The interventions of the two latter take quite different forms, but in their effect they are identical.

Manannán mac Lir

Whatever of the Celts as a whole, whose original homeland lay landlocked and far from the ocean, it would be strange had the Irish, whose fortunes were so permanently bound up with the seas around them, not known a god who claimed the sea for his special realm. In fact the indications are that they may have known several such deities, but of these the only one adequately documented is Manannán mac Lir, whose patronymic means literally 'son of the sea'. His name is related to that of the Isle of Man, and the waters with which he is particularly associated are those between north-east Ireland and Britain. He had, moreover, a near namesake in Britain: the names Manannán mac Lir and Manawydan fab Llŷr form a close, though not an exact, correspondence.

In the earlier texts Manannán is not specifically numbered among the gods of the Tuatha Dé and he is not mentioned in the tales of the two

battles of Magh Tuiredh. Whether this differentiation is original or merely springs from his functional specialisaton as god of the sea is not certain, but it is worth noting that another god connected with the sea, the rather shadowy Tethra, does take part in the Second Battle of Magh Tuiredh, but on the opposite side to the Tuatha Dé. Like Manannán, Tethra was also known as lord of the joyous otherworld.

It is in fact the legend of the sea-journey to the joyous otherworld that has established Manannán's image in Irish literature. In the *Voyage of Bran*, which was probably composed in the late seventh century, he travels over the sea in his chariot and addresses the mortal voyager Bran in words which express vividly the inversion of reality which characterises the otherworld vision of things:

It seems to Bran a wondrous beauty
in his curragh on a clear sea;
while to me in my chariot from afar
it is a flowery plain on which I ride.

What is a clear sea
for the prowed craft in which Bran
*   is,*
is a Plain of Delights with profusion
*   of flowers*
for me in my two-wheeled chariot.

Bran sees
a host of waves breaking across the
*   clear sea:*
I myself see in Magh Mon
red-tipped flowers without blemish.

Sea-horses glisten in summer
as far as Bran's eye can stretch;
flowers pour forth a stream of
*   honey*
in the land of Manannán son of
*   Ler . . .*

Speckled salmon leap from the
*   womb*
of the white sea on which you look;
they are calves, they are bright-
*   coloured lambs,*
at peace, without mutual hostility
*   . . .*

It is along the top of a wood
that your tiny craft has sailed across
*   the ridges,*
a beautiful wood with its harvest of
*   fruit*
under the prow of your little boat.

A wood with blossom and fruit
and on it the true fragrance of the
*   vine;*
a wood without decay or death,
with leaves the colour of gold . . .

Elsewhere Manannán is 'the rider of the crested sea', the waves are his steeds, and when the sea is agitated 'the tresses of Manannán's wife are tossed'. His traditional home is the Isle of Man – conceived less as a geographical reality than as a terrestrial location of the otherworld – but he is also associated with the supernatural island of Emhain Abhlach, 'Emhain of the Apple-trees', which the literature identifies with the Isle of Arran in the Firth of Clyde and of which the title is echoed in that of King Arthur's Avalon. In later texts he is explicitly included among the Tuatha Dé, and in one of them he leads King Cormac mac Airt from Tara to his otherworld court – which by implication is near at hand in Ireland – just as Lugh had led there

Right. Head, evidently of a Gaulish divinity, from Nine, commune of Lectoure. Musée Municipal, Lectoure.

Opposite. View in profile of a head which may be that of a Gaulish divinity, from Caillavet, commune of Lectoure. Musée Municipal, Lectoure.

Cormac's grandfather, Conn 'of the Hundred Battles'. At the same time an attempt was made among the *literati* to transform Manannán into a historical character and already *c.*A.D. 900 Cormac mac Cuilennáin in his Glossary turns him into a marvellous merchant and skilled navigator who lived in the Isle of Man and who was later deified by the Irish and the Britons. But far from concealing Manannán's divinity, this merely confirms what we have otherwise good reasons to assume, namely that Manannán and his British counterpart Manawydan represent a single deity who was known and honoured both in Britain and in Ireland.

Above. Trio of hooded deities (*genii cucullati*) from Housesteads, Northumberland. These mysterious hooded deities seem to be associated with fertility, but their significance remains largely a matter for speculation. Museum of Antiquities, Newcastle upon Tyne.

Right. A god holding a torc, from Rodez (Aveyron). The hair, which is not visible in this front view, is formed with the characteristic spirals of La Tène art. Musée Fenaille, Rodez.

Opposite. Enamelled human figure forming the handle of an Irish bowl found in a Viking tomb in Miklebostad, Norway. Historisk Museum, Bergen.

71

The Gods of Britain

The centre-piece of medieval Welsh literature and the most celebrated example of Welsh storytelling is the Four Branches of the *Mabinogi*. These four tales, the work of an accomplished and sensitive author-redactor of the late eleventh century, have as their protagonists the gods of Welsh and British tradition. At the same time their testimony is not easy to interpret. For one thing, far from drawing upon the rich resources of an integrated mythology, the indications are that the author of the Four Branches and the storytellers whose work he inherited had at their disposal only the scattered residue of a fragmented and half-forgotten tradition, and this they interwove with a succession of international story-motifs to produce finally the extant narrative. And despite the skill of the final author-redactor the plots of some of the tales still betray their composite character by numerous obscurities and inconsistencies. By reason of this repeated reworking of the material and the continual assimilation of extraneous story-elements, it is not easy to isolate extended patterns of narrative which can reasonably be ascribed to British mythological tradition. There are undoubtedly many elements that derive from that tradition – the sojourn in the happy otherworld, the raid on the otherworld, the waste land, the otherworld lord soliciting the aid of a human hero, etc. – and these can frequently be supplemented from other Welsh texts and from the more abundant resources of Irish literature. It has also been argued that the Fourth Branch of the *Mabinogi, Math vab Mathonwy* 'Math son of Mathonwy', preserves an archaic narrative complex.

The Family of Dôn

Math son of Mathonwy is largely concerned with a group of characters sometimes referred to as the family of Dôn. It is told of Math son of Mathonwy, lord of Gwynedd in north Wales, that he had a certain peculiarity: he must always have his feet resting in a virgin's lap, 'unless the turmoil of war prevented him', presumably because she embodied the vital and undiminished source of fertility with which he must maintain constant and harmonious contact so as to ensure the fruitful discharge of his royal function. His foot-holder at that time was the fair Goewin and, unknown to him, his sister's son, Gilfaethwy son of Dôn, was pining for love of her. Gilfaethwy confided in his brother Gwydion and the latter then contrived by a combination of trickery and magic to instigate war between Math and Pryderi son of Pwyll, the lord of south Wales. While Math was thus absent, Gilfaethwy slept with Goewin against her will. When Math eventually returned and learned of the dishonour done to him he struck his nephews with his magic wand and turned them into a stag and a hind. They remained in this form for a year, during a second year they were wild boar and wild sow, and for a third year they were wolves. Then they were restored to human form. Subsequently when Math sought a new foot-holder, Gwydion suggested his sister Arianrhod daughter of Dôn. She is brought in and asked to step over the magic wand as a test of her virginity, but as she does so, she

Intaglio showing the north-British deity Cocidius, equated to Silvanus the hunter. Museum of Antiquities. Newcastle upon Tyne.

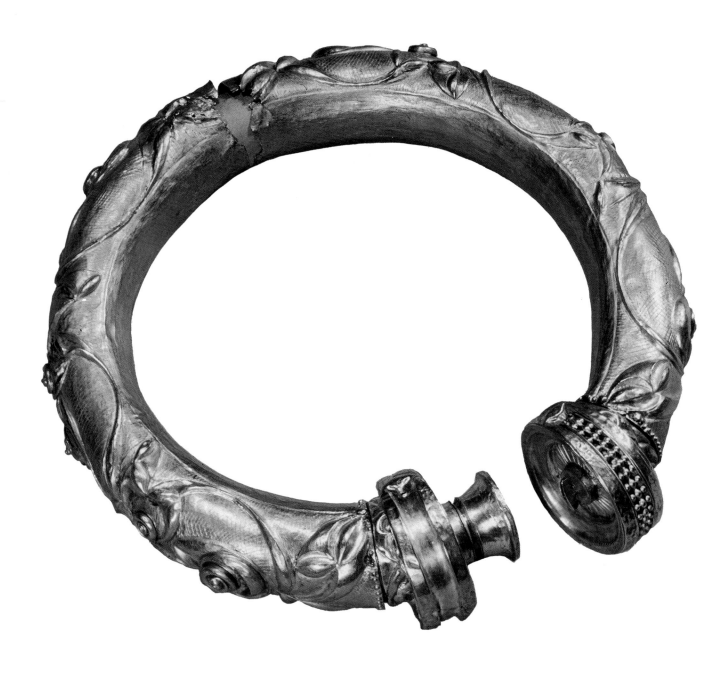

drops a yellow-haired boy as well as something else which Gwydion picks up and conceals in a chest. The boy is baptized Dylan and immediately he makes for the sea and takes on its nature, and from this he is known henceforth as Dylan Eil Don, 'Dylan son of Wave'.

The object which Gwydion concealed turns out to be a second male child, and it is with his fate that the rest of the tale concerns itself. In her shame and dismay Arianrhod swears that her son will not have a name until she gives him one, but through Gwydion's ingenuity and magic she is led all unwittingly to name him Lleu Llaw Gyffes, 'The Bright One of the Skilful Hand'. Later she swears that he will never bear arms until she equips him, and again she is tricked into undoing her own interdiction. Finally she swears that he will never have a wife of humankind. Gwydion takes counsel with Math and together they conjure a wife for Lleu from the flowers of the oak, the broom and the meadowsweet, and they call her Blodeuwedd, 'Flower-aspect'. But though Blodeuwedd was the fairest maiden that mortal ever saw, she was not the most faithful. With her lover,

A large gold torc or collar from Broighter, Limavady, Co. Derry, late first century B.C. The ornament consists of spirals, trumpet patterns, lentoid bosses, etc. It is clear that torcs had a socio-religious significance and they are worn by the images of deities. They were also worn by princely heroes: according to the early Welsh poem 'The Gododdin' the three hundred warriors who went to their death in the fight at Catraeth were all of them 'gold-torced'. National Museum of Ireland, Dublin.

Bronze shield boss found in the River Thames at Wandsworth, London, and dating from the first or second century B.C. Two elaborately extended birds, each a mirror image of the other, fill the circular area around the central protuberance. Wings and beaks are engraved with tiny motifs, the whole composition 'illustrating the combination of plastic and graphic which is a particular feature of insular Celtic art'. British Museum, London.

Gronw Pebyr, she plots to kill Lleu who is wounded and flies away in the form of an eagle. Eventually Gwydion seeks him out and restores him to human form. Blodeuwedd he turns into an owl, the outcast among the birds, and Gronw is slain by Lleu.

Professor Georges Dumézil has demonstrated from other Indo-European traditions that complex mythological sequences may long outlast the religious ideologies which engendered them, provided they have already been cast in a literary form that guarantees their survival. The first half of *Math vab Mathonwy* he would regard as just such a text, and in the interaction of the several members of the family of Dôn presented there he traces out, ingeniously but convincingly, a British reflex of the ancient Indo-European social ideology of the three functions which we have already referred to briefly on page 60.

Scattered references in medieval poetry and prose presuppose the existence of a substantial body of tradition about the family of Dôn that is only partly reflected in the *Mabinogi*; thus *Culhwch and Olwen* refers incidentally to Amaethon son of Dôn – whose name means literally 'great, or divine, ploughman' – as the only one who could till a certain piece of land in a miraculously short time. The antiquity of this body of tradition is evident – as indeed is its common Celticity. Lleu, the counterpart of Irish Lugh and Gaulish 'Mercury', retains certain traces of the god of skill and craftsmanship, and Math and Gwydion are distinguished by their magical powers. This association with magic, which seems to hold for the 'children' of Dôn as a body or

confraternity, is reminiscent of the traditional notion of the Tuatha Dé Danann, and it has been suggested that Welsh Dôn is the equivalent of Irish *Donu* (the original form of the name Danann), 'the mother of the gods'. Despite the disparity in nomenclature – Lugh-Lleu and Goibhniu-Gofannon provide the only correspondences – it seems probable that the family of Dôn derive from the same system of Celtic gods as is represented by the Irish Tuatha Dé Danann.

The Family of Llŷr

The Second Branch, *Branwen Daughter of Llŷr*, introduces the three members of the family of Llŷr: Branwen, Bendigeidfran ('Brân the Blessed') and Manawydan, though it is only in the Third Branch that Manawydan comes to play an independent role. In the story which bears her name Branwen is in reality a rather minor character, the passive victim of injustice and tragic circumstance, and the whole tale is dominated by the enormous figure of Bendigeidfran. He gives his sister in marriage to Matholwch, king of Ireland, but she is subsequently humiliated and ill-treated

there and Bendigeidfran sets out with an army of the Men of Britain to exact revenge from the Irish. Such is his gigantic stature that, while his followers sail to Ireland in ships, he simply wades alongside them. The subsequent narrative reaches its climax in a fierce battle between the Irish and the Britons. The Irish have a magic cauldron into which they cast their slain so that they rise on the morrow as good fighting men as before, and it is only when one of their number succeeds in destroying the cauldron that the Britons prevail. Even then theirs is a Pyrrhic victory and of all their heroes only seven survive beside Bendigeidfran, who has been wounded in the foot by a poisonous spear. (His wound no doubt corresponds to that which incapacitated Bron the Fisher King and other related characters of Arthurian romance for whom he was evidently the prototype.) He commands the seven to cut off his head and carry it with them to the White Mount in London and to bury it there so as to protect the kingdom against invasion. They execute his order and set out for London bearing with them his severed head. On the way they spend

seven years at Harlech feasting and listening to the music of the magic birds of Rhiannon, and eighty years on the island of Gwales in the peace and joy of the happy otherworld. And – here appears the motif of the living head which is almost a commonplace in Celtic tradition – during all this time Bendigeidfran's head remained uncorrupted and provided them with as pleasant company as he himself had done when alive.

Unlike the 'children' of Dôn there is no evidence that the Llŷr family ever comprised an extensive system of divinities, and of its three attested members it is not even certain that

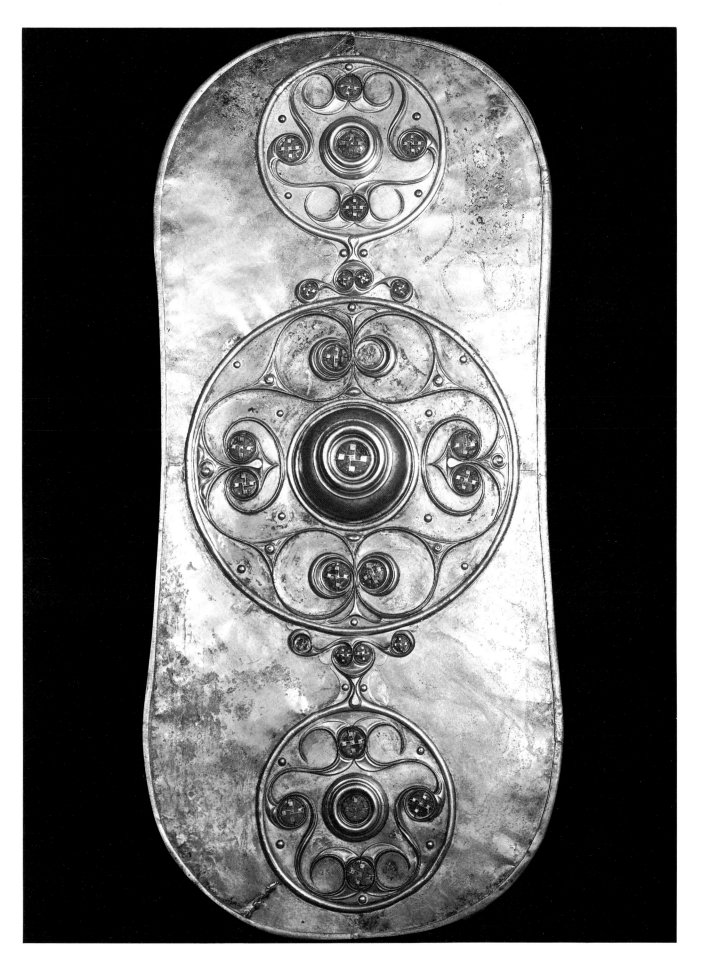

Pwyll, Rhiannon and Pryderi

The First Branch of the *Mabinogi* falls into two sections. The opening section draws upon the common Celtic notion that otherworld rulers sometimes invoke the intervention of mortals in their mutual conflicts. In this instance the mortal is Pwyll, lord of Dyfed in southwest Wales, and he slays the enemy of Arawn, king of Annwn. In recognition of this exploit he is henceforth known as Pwyll 'the Head of Annwn'. Since, however, Annwn is a traditional name for the otherworld, it has been assumed that Pwyll was originally a deity. His name means literally 'wisdom', an apt title for the all-knowing god of the otherworld – it may be recalled that one of the Daghdha's titles describes him as 'The Mighty One of Great Knowledge'.

The closing section is centred upon the birth of the hero Pryderi. Pwyll, having returned to his own kingdom, encounters the lady Rhiannon riding a white horse and in circumstances which leave no doubt as to her supernatural provenance. They marry and from their union Pryderi is born. But on the night of his birth he is mysteriously abducted, is later found by Teyrnon, lord of Gwent Is-coed, and is reared by him and his wife for several years until, realising that he is the lost son of Pwyll and Rhiannon, they restore him to his rightful parents. When Pwyll dies, Pryderi succeeds to the lordship of Dyfed, and then later on, in the Third Branch of the *Mabinogi*, Rhiannon becomes the wife of Manawydan.

These are but the salient facts of a

Branwen can claim any great antiquity. On the other hand, the association of Brân (as Bendigeidfran was known earlier) and Manawydan is old: there was evidently a tradition that they were sister's sons to Beli Mawr, 'Beli the Great', an ancestor-deity from whom several of the royal lines of Wales claimed descent, and an early verse reference represents them as presiding together over the otherworld and its feast. It is therefore a rather remarkable fact that the early Irish poetic account of Bran's voyage to the otherworld links this Irish Bran with Manannán, particularly since the central theme of the Welsh tale seems originally to have been a raid on the otherworld, here terrestrially located in Ireland. But Irish literature does not know a god Bran and the hero of the voyage-tale is a mere mortal; consequently one cannot lightly assume the pairing of

Manannán and Bran is to be identified with that of Manawydan and Brân. As for Manawydan, his name and patronymic equate him with Manannán, but not his legend. In the Third Branch he is portrayed as a man of patience, wise counsel and ready resource, but nowhere is there any clear indication that he was thought of as a god of the sea. It can hardly be doubted that he and Manannán derive from a deity known to both branches of the insular Celts, but their legends must subsequently have diverged very considerably and in the case of Manawydan they have probably been drastically reshaped by late redactors. One notable parallel remains, however, for just as Manannán tends to stand apart from the Irish Tuatha Dé Danann, so Manawydan is differentiated from the British family of Dôn. This may well reflect an ancient distinction.

close and complicated narrative which reveals only tantalising glimpses of the underlying mythology. The form and meaning of Teyrnon's name (from earlier *Tigernonos*, 'Great, or Divine, Lord') imply divinity and also a role more important than is actually his in the tale. Rhiannon (from *Rigantona*, 'Great, or Divine, Queen') would appear from certain details of the extant tale to have had equine associations and

some have thought to identify her with Epona, the horse-goddess. It is also tempting to equate Rhiannon and Pryderi with Modron, the 'Great (Divine) Mother', and Mabon, the 'Great Son', who 'was taken away when three nights old from his mother'. But here, as in other parts of the *Mabinogi*, the evidence lends itself to speculation rather than to confident conclusions and one finds oneself ultimately compelled to echo critic and

poet Matthew Arnold's sentiment: 'The very first thing that strikes one, in reading the *Mabinogion*, is how evidently the mediaeval story-teller is pillaging an antiquity of which he does not fully possess the secret; he is like a peasant building his hut on the site of Halicarnassus or Ephesus; he builds, but what he builds is full of materials of which he knows not the history, or knows by a glimmering tradition only.'

Above. Fleshfork decorated with ravens and swans, from Dunaverney, Ireland. Irish legal and literary texts mention fleshfork and cauldron together as important items of a person's household goods. In the Old Irish tale 'The Story of Mac Da Thó's Pig', there is the following account of the five great banqueting halls (*bruidhnea*) of Ireland, which are in fact specialised representations of the otherworld: 'There were seven doors in each hall, seven roads through it, and seven fireplaces therein. There were seven cauldrons, with an ox and a salted pig in each of them. And the person who came that way would thrust the fleshfork into the cauldron, and whatever he obtained with the first thrust he ate, and if he obtained nothing at the first attempt, then he did not get a second.' British Museum, London.

Opposite below. The white horse cut in the chalk scarp at Uffington, Oxfordshire, England, close to a pre-existing Iron-Age hill-fort. It is thought to have been the work of Belgic settlers during the first century B.C. Most likely it had a cultic significance and the suggestion is that it marks a sacred site associated with a horse-goddess such as Epona.

Left. The horse-goddess Epona on a relief from Kastel, Germany. She carries an object, perhaps a fruit of some kind, in her right hand. Rheinisches Landesmuseum, Bonn.

The Goddesses of the Insular Celts

The name of these twin hills in Co. Kerry was Dá Chích Anann, 'The Paps of Anu', and they are still referred to in English as 'The Paps'. The goddess Anu, or Danu, was known as the mother of the gods, and under the former title she was identified especially with the province of Munster, with its land and its fertility.

Medhbh of Connacht

Early in the present century a distinguished Celticist wrote a scathing commentary on the morals of the ancient Irish, basing his remarks on the evidence of the early sagas. He dealt at particular length with the legendary queen Medhbh of Connacht, she who led her armies against Ulster in the saga of *Táin Bó Cuailnge,* and it is indeed true that Medhbh's sexual capacity receives considerable emphasis in the literature. As well as being the paramour of the prodigiously virile hero Ferghus mac Roich and others, she is said to have claimed that 'never was she without one man in the shadow of another' and to have always sought a husband 'without niggardliness, without jealousy and without fear'. But Medhbh's legend is not a historical document, nor indeed is she herself the historical personage she purports to be. In fact this is one of the not infrequent instances where bad morals make good mythology, and it is precisely in her breaches of propriety that we find the most obvious evidence of Medhbh's

divinity; her licentiousness is merely the literary expression of one of the characteristic functions of the Celtic goddess.

It has often been remarked that the Celts had no goddess of love, no Venus or Aphrodite, though on the other hand the majority of their goddesses display a vigorous sexuality. Similarly, early Irish offers surprisingly little literature of love in the conventional sense: it is true that it has numerous tales of 'wooings', 'elopements', etc., but these deal with the circumstances of the erotic encounter rather than with the personal relationship involved. The poetry of passionate love may very well have existed in popular song (which is practically unattested for the early period), but in the mainstream of Irish literary tradition it receives only the barest recognition. It is not unlikely indeed that the two phenomena – the literary and the mythological – are connected. Since the heroines of the love-tales are for the most part divine, it is natural then that the narratives should reflect the mythological

role of love, which is of its nature functional or ritual rather than personal, and in point of fact it is only in the hands of the monastic *littérateurs* and under the influence of foreign romantic *genres* that the personal and psychological aspects of love are gradually more fully elaborated.

The mythological role of love and sexuality is bound up primarily with the character of the Irish goddess as divine mother and personification of the land. The cult of mother-goddess is attested in Gaul from prehistoric times. It may also have preceded the Celts in Ireland, and equally it may have accompanied them there, but in any event its presence is hardly in doubt. The divine people, the Tuatha Dé, were reputed to be the family or

Opposite. Mother-goddess holding a child, from Prunay-le-Gillon. Musée des Antiquités Nationales, St Germain-en-Laye.

Below. Goddesses from High Rochester (Bremenium), Northumberland. Museum of Antiquities, Newcastle upon Tyne.

descendants of the goddess Danu, as the Welsh gods were said to be issued from Dôn (or the Indian from Aditi), and Wales, like Gaul, had its 'Great Mother' *Modron*. In Irish literature Danu is frequently confused with Anu, who is described in Cormac's Glossary as the mother of the Irish gods, *mater deorum Hibernensium*, and in the *Cóir Anmann* ('Fitness of Names') as the goddess of prosperity, to whom the province of Munster owed its wealth and fertility. Anu's identification with the earth is brought out even more explicitly in the name of a Kerry mountain, 'The Paps of Anu', *Dá Chích Anann*.

But this equation of the goddess and the earth is normally defined and limited by local affiliations. At its most extensive it comprises the domain of the cultural nation, in other words the land of Ireland, in which sense it is most clearly exemplified in the trio of divine eponyms, Ériu, Fódla and Banbha, who reigned over Ireland at the coming of the Gaels. In general, however, the innumerable goddesses known to tradition tend to be associated with certain localities – a province, a district, a river, or a particular place – and modern folklore still retains vivid memories of fairy queens such as *Áine* who had her seat at Cnoc Áine in county Limerick, *Aoibheall* of Craig Liath in Clare and *Clíodna* of Carraig Clíodna in Cork. The significant point is that in these instances the ruler of the supernatural realm is a goddess rather than a god, precisely as in those early Irish tales which represent the otherworld as 'The Land of Women'. It is evidently an old tradition and one which proved remarkably tenacious, and it seems to confirm that the notion of a great goddess who was mother of the gods is a basic element of insular Celtic mythology. One consequence of this priority is that the goddess often assumes a dominating role vis-à-vis her male partners. An obvious instance is Medhbh, whose husbands are never more than sleeping partners. Another, expressed in more graphic terms, is the monstrous couple who appear in several of the early tales and whose appearance is on each occasion fraught with evil consequence. In Táin Bó Cuailnge the woman rides while her husband walks and, when they are challenged by Cú Chulainn, it is she who answers in his stead. In *Branwen* the man is described as huge and terrible in appearance, but despite his size his wife is twice as big. The legend ascribes to her two of the common attributes of the Celtic goddess: fertility and warlike vigour, and her name appears to confirm the combination: *Cymidei Cymeinfoll*, 'Big-bellied Battler(?)'.

Goddesses of War

The warlike propensity of the goddess is variously expressed. There is the quasi-historical Medhbh, ruthless commander-in-chief of the armies which she sends against Ulster – her very appearance deprived warriors of two-thirds of their valour. There are Amazonian teachers of the martial arts like *Buanann*, 'The Lasting One', 'mother of heroes', and *Scáthach*, 'The Shadowy One', who ran finishing schools for young heroes. It was under Scáthach's tutelage that Cú Chulainn acquired the special skills that later extricated him from many dangerous situations. Above all there is a formidable group who have a special claim to the title of goddess of war. Though often appearing singly these are normally conceived of as a trio. They generally comprise the *Morríghan*, 'Phantom Queen', and *Badhbh*, 'Crow, Raven', accompanied by *Nemhain*, 'Frenzy' or by *Macha*. Since these goddesses are not infrequently identified with one another, the inference is that they are really the triplication of a single deity, and this is in fact corroborated by occasional references to the three Morríghans. That they were known throughout the Celtic world is virtually certain: the *Cathubodua*, 'crow, raven of battle', attested in Haute-Savoie corresponds to the Irish *Badhbh Chatha* and the notion of the trio of furies recurs in Britain in the Benwell inscription *Lamiis Tribus*, 'To the Three Lamiae'. In Wales the river-name Aeron (from Celtic *Agronā*, 'goddess of slaughter')

points to parallel traditions, and a legend of the Washer at the Ford has survived there which closely resembles that of the Morríghan and the Daghdha in the battle of Magh Tuiredh (see page 66). And no doubt one should also include in this formidable gallery the goddess *Andraste* whom the British queen Boudica invoked before going into battle.

Normally these war-goddesses do not themselves engage in armed conflict: their weapons are the magic they command and the very terror which they inspire by their dread presence. Before the battle of Magh Tuiredh the Morríghan undertakes to aid the Daghdha by depriving the leader of the Fomhoire of 'the blood of his heart and the kidneys of his courage'. They constantly change form and often haunt the battlefield in the form of hooded crows. At one point in *Táin Bó Cuailnge* a beautiful young woman approaches Cú Chulainn, declares her love for him and offers him her wealth and cattle. But he replies that this is a time for fighting, not for love-making, adding rather ungraciously that in any case he has no wish to be helped by a woman. The young woman, who is really the Morríghan, then reverts to type and warns Cú Chulainn that she will attack him while he is engaged in single combat, first in the form of an eel, next as a grey wolf, and finally as a hornless red heifer. In the event, she carries out her threat, and Cú Chulainn barely escapes with his life.

Nemhain, as her name implies, is she who creates panic among the fighting men: when she raised her cry over the armies facing Cú Chulainn, 'a hundred warriors of them fell dead that night of terror and fright'.

Macha

Macha has been mentioned as one of the trio of war-goddesses. She is in fact one of three namesakes known to Irish tradition, all of which were

evidently manifestations of the deity who gave her name to Emhain Mhacha, capital of the ancient province of Ulster, and to Ard Macha (Armagh), the future centre of Christian Ireland. She is one of a number of mythical women – Carman and Tailtiu are others – in whose honour annual assemblies or festivals were held after their death. Some of them are warlike in character and most of them are associated with some form of violence or duress, but they are also connected in one way or another with the cultivation of land and its fertility and their assemblies generally coincide with Lughnasadh, the great festival of harvest-time dedicated to Lugh.

The first of the Machas was wife of Nemhedh, 'The Sacred One', who was the leader of the third of the invasions recounted in *Leabhar Gabhála*. She foresaw in a vision the destruction and dissension which would result from the great 'Cattle-Raid of Cuailnge' *(Táin Bó Cuailnge)* and her heart broke within her. She died in one of the twelve plains cleared by her husband and for that reason it was named after her.

The second Macha ruled over Ireland alone for a time and repelled by force those who contested her sovereignty. She then took one of her two rivals, Cimbaeth, in marriage, dominating him as Medhbh dominated Ailill. And when the five sons of another claimant continued to oppose her, she sought them out in their hunting ground, enticed them one by one into the forest to lie with her, and there bound each in turn. After reducing them to servitude, she forced them to build the royal fort of Emhain Mhacha.

The last of the three Machas recalls the familiar theme of the supernatural bride who lives happily with her mortal husband until in a moment of indiscretion he violates a promise not to mention her name in the concourse of men. One day a beautiful young woman walked into the house of Crunnchu, a wealthy husbandman of Ulster and a widower. Without speaking any word, she attended to the household duties, and, when night came, she made the ritual right-hand

turn *(for dessel)* to ensure good fortune and entered Crunnchu's bed. She became pregnant by him and through their union his wealth was increased. In due course Crunnchu went to the great assembly of the Ulstermen. He had been warned by his wife not to speak of her there, but when he saw the king's horses racing and heard the poets and the public sounding their praises, he forgot the warning and boasted that his wife could outrun them. The king took up the challenge; the woman was summoned and, despite her protestations that her time had almost come, she was compelled to run against the royal horses. She finished before them, but there she cried out in pain and gave birth to twins (Irish *emhain*), whence the name of Emhain Mhacha. And before she died from her anguish and exhaustion she laid a curse on the Ulstermen: until the end of nine generations in times of greatest peril the Ulstermen would experience the same malady as she, so that every

grown man would be as weak as a woman in childbed. And so it happened that when Medhbh attacked Ulster, its heroes lay prostrate and it fell to Cú Chulainn to defend the province alone against the might of Connacht.

Two features stand out in these legends which we have already noted in connection with the Irish goddesses: first an association with the land and with the idea of fertility throughout animate and inanimate nature, and secondly the assertion of authority by martial prowess. But on closer scrutiny it will be seen that they offer one of the most impressive evidences in Irish literature for Georges Dumézil's view that Indo-European socio-religious ideology was based upon a conceptual system comprising three primary functions: the first relating to magic and religion, the second to warrior activities, and the third to wealth and fertility (see page 60). Of the three Machas one is a visionary, another is a warrior, while

the third is the telluric *materfamilias* who brings with her increase and fruitfulness. The neat collocation of these three roles in the one goddess can hardly be accidental, but seems rather to reveal the shaping hand of the druidic theologian.

As for Macha's contest with the racing horses this may reflect an ancient rite, as has been suggested, and provides an apparent link with the Celtic horse-goddess Epona and Rhiannon, who is her probable Welsh equivalent.

Goddesses of the Happy Otherworld

In the frequent tales and poems which concern themselves especially with the marvels and delights of the happy otherworld, there is naturally a tendency to dwell on those aspects of the goddess which are aesthetically most pleasing. This genre of composition was most actively cultivated at a time when the lyric impulse was young and vigorous, and this fact has influenced the delineation of the supernatural

heroine. Conla son of Conn of the Hundred Battles is visited by 'a young and beautiful woman of noble race whom neither death awaits nor old age' and enticed by her to that delightful land where 'there are none but women and girls'. Bran son of Febhal is similarly persuaded by a woman bearing a branch from the apple-tree of Emhnae, which was of silver with white blossoms. The goddess Clíodna, as she appeared to Tadhg son of Cian, was remarkably beautiful and the noblest and most desirable of the women of the whole world. She had three brightly coloured birds which fed on the apples of the otherworld tree and sang so sweetly that they would soothe the sick to sleep. These correspond to the three birds of Rhiannon and may also bear some relation to the birds which are sometimes shown perched upon the shoulders of a goddess in Gaulish sculpture.

In the story of 'The Wasting Sickness of Cú Chulainn' (*Serglighe Con*

Fragment of a lintel from Nages (Gard) decorated by two severed heads and two galloping horses. Musée Archéologique, Nîmes.

Culainn) Fann and Lí Ban ('Beauty of Women') conform to the general idea of feminine beauty and grace, but nevertheless they betray a touch of temper that shows they are ultimately from the same stable as Macha and Medhbh. One day Cú Chulainn tries, and fails, to capture two magic lake-birds for his wife, who wished to have one of them for each shoulder (like the Gaulish goddess). He falls asleep then, and in his dream two women come and beat him with horse-whips, so that when he awakes he is unable to speak and lies prostrate for a year. Eventually he is restored to health, is persuaded by his supernatural chastisers to offer his aid in arms to their king, and thereafter he tastes of the delights that normally await the mortal hero invited to the otherworld.

Above. Standing stones, Cloghane, Co. Kerry. Such stones, known as *galláin* in Irish, occur singly or in alignments as at Cloghane. They were pagan monuments used especially to mark boundaries and burial places, and not infrequently they came to be regarded as memorials of famous legendary events.

Opposite left. Portion of the famous calendar found at Coligny, near Bourg (Ain), at the end of last century. Inscribed upon a sheet of bronze, it constitutes by far the oldest extensive document in a Celtic language: a date in the early first century A.D. or late first century B.C. has been suggested. It uses Roman lettering and numeration, but its content is quite independent of the Roman calendar, and the presumption is that it was drawn up by the Gaulish druids. It marks each month either by the abbreviation MAT, 'good', or by ANM, 'not good', a distinction which apparently extends to the days of the month as well. This is perhaps illustrated by Irish tradition, where the druids are sometimes called upon to decide whether or not a particular day is propitious for some serious enterprise, such as taking up arms or being born into the world. Thus we read of the mothers of famous kings artificially delaying their delivery until the auspicious time so as to ensure the future greatness of their offspring, and we find the young Cú Chulainn taking up arms because he hears the druid Cathbhadh prophesy that he who takes up arms on that day shall have a short life with eternal fame. Musée des Beaux-Arts, Lyons.

Opposite above right. Loughcrew, Co. Meath, site of an important passage-grave cemetery. These megalithic tombs were sometimes ascribed by tradition to the activities of the supernatural beings, or goddesses, known as *caillecha*, 'hags': part of the Loughcrew site is known as *Sliabh na Caillighe*, 'The Hag's Mountain'.

Édaín

It is in this congenial company that the goddess Édaín fits most easily, though her legend – one of the most fascinating in Irish literature – is not directly concerned with this Elysian otherworld. It is a story in three parts. In the beginning Oenghus, In Mac Óg, woos Édaín Echraidhe daugher of Ailill, the loveliest maiden in Ireland, on behalf of Midhir, lord of the *sídh* of Brí Léith. But when Midhir returns home with his bride, his first wife Fuamhnach, a woman of great cunning and magic, strikes her with a rod and changes her into a pool of water. The water turns into a worm, and the worm into a purple fly of great size and radiant beauty that fills the air with music and fragrance. 'Midhir knew that it was Édaín that was in that form, and so long as that fly attended upon him, he never took to himself a wife and the sight of her was his nourishment. He would fall asleep to her humming, and whenever anyone approached who did not love him, she would awaken him.' Fuamhnach then raised a magic wind which carried Édaín out upon the rocks and waves of the sea where she was buffeted about for seven weary years. She was then found by Oenghus and maintained by him in a beautiful crystal sun-bower. But once again Fuamhnach intervened and drove her abroad until in the end she fell into

the golden drinking cup of the wife of Édar, a champion of Ulster. The woman swallowed her and she was duly reborn as Édaín daughter of Édar a thousand and twelve years after her birth as Ailill's daughter.

The two succeeding tales are concerned with Midhir's constant endeavours to recover Édaín. When Eochaidh Airemh becomes king of Ireland he dispatches messengers to seek out the most beautiful girl in the land. They find Édaín daughter of Édar and he marries her. Later she is approached by Midhir who explains that she was once his wife and asks her to return to him; but she refuses unless it be with Eochaidh's consent. Midhir then visits Ailill and they play at 'chess'. After losing three games and forfeiting high stakes, Midhir wins the fourth and when asked his wish says simply: 'My arms around Édaín and a kiss from her.' A month from that day he returns to claim his prize. Eochaidh has the royal house of Tara ringed by armed men and the doors are locked – but his precautions are in vain: as soon as Midhir is permitted to embrace Édaín, he rises through the roof-window of the house bearing her with him, and they are last seen flying away in the form of two swans. Eochaidh and the men of Ireland set out in pursuit and, fortified by their discovery of certain magic procedures, they begin to dig up Midhir's own residence, the *sídh* of Brí Léith. Midhir comes forth and promises to restore Édaín, but in the event fifty women appear, all of like form and raiment as Édaín. Eochaidh's problem is that of Damayantī in the Indian *Mahābārata*, but whereas Damayantī successfully identified Nala among the gods who had assumed his appearance, Eochaidh was less fortunate: only much later does he discover that the girl he has chosen is not Édaín, but her daughter – and his. From this incest was born one of the celebrated kings of Irish legend, Conaire Mór.

In its complete form this tale has a strange, haunting quality and a sense of timelessness which are no doubt attributable in some measure to the fact that it moves as it were between

Above. The mother-goddesses, from Cirencester, Gloucestershire. Two of them hold trays of fruit, the third a tray of cakes or loaves. Corinium Museum, Cirencester.

two worlds. Eochaidh is here represented as a mortal king and lover vying with a supernatural rival, and – in keeping with a common feature of Irish tradition – the mortal can here mount an offensive against the gods and subdue them by main force and by magic, but especially the latter, for magic is a potent instrument in whatever hands and one to which even the gods must sometimes yield. Eochaidh's bride, the reborn Édaín, is described as the daughter of an Ulster champion, whereas the narrative reveals her clearly as one of the immortal race of the gods. For example, it is stated that Eochaidh became king and that in the following year he commanded the men of Ireland to hold the feast of Tara in order to assess their tributes and taxes. But they replied that they would not convene the feast for a king that had no queen, and this is why he instituted the search that led to his marriage to Édaín. In the context of Irish tradition the meaning of this is clear:

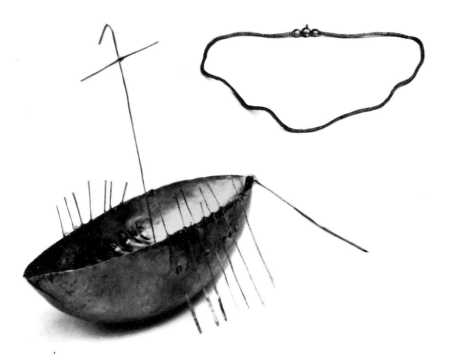

Eochaidh had become king, but his kingship could be validated only by his union with the goddess of sovereignty, in this case Édaín. This union of king and goddess was at one time ritually enacted at the Feast of Tara.

The Goddess of Sovereignty

The notion of a mystical or symbolic union between the king and his kingdom is older than Indo-European society. And where the kingdom was conceived anthropomorphically as a goddess, the latter then symbolised not merely the soil and substance of its territory, but also the spiritual and legal dominion which the king exercised over it, in other words his sovereignty. Nowhere was this divine image of sovereignty visualised so clearly as among the Celts, and more especially in Ireland, where it remained a remarkably evocative and compelling concept for as long as native tradition lasted. For obvious reasons it will be more convenient to discuss its mytho-historical role when we come to deal with the notion of sacral kingship, but this should not be allowed to obscure the fact that it is closely implicated in all the various epiphanies of the Celtic goddess already referred to; in a sense it is the factor which integrates them into a single unity. We have seen that the Irish, and indeed the Celtic, goddess

is primarily concerned with the prosperity of the land: its fertility, its animal life, and (when it is conceived as a political unit) its security against external forces. All the seemingly contradictory characters of the deity – maternal, seasonal, warlike, young or aged, beautiful or monstrous – may be referred to this fundamental nexus, and it is significant that, in general, each individual goddess reveals several or all of these characters, and even though one of them may predominate, the others are rarely absent. Thus Anu, who is explicitly described as a goddess of plenty, is sometimes identified with the Morríghan, the war-goddess *par excellence,* and the Morríghan, like Anu, was commemorated in a placename ('The Paps of the Morríghan') that testified to her maternal function.

Equally complex, and more fully documented, is the legend of the Caillech Bhérri, 'The Hag of Bérre', who is as famous in modern Irish folklore as she evidently was in the early literary tradition. Her epithet connects her with a peninsula in the south-west of Ireland, but her associations in folklore extend throughout Ireland and Gaelic Scotland, and it is related of her that 'she dropped cairns on to hills in Meath out of her apron, was responsible for moving islands in west Kerry, built mountains from rocks

carried in her creel in Scotland, and was queen of the Limerick fairies'. The geotectonic role thus ascribed to her is an expression of her intimate connection with the land, and accords well with other traditions which picture her as a divine ancestress of numerous progeny and as an epitome of longevity who had passed repeatedly through the cycle of youth and age. 'She entered upon seven periods of youth', says an early note, 'so that every husband used to pass from her to death through old age, and so that her grand-children and great-grand-children were peoples and races.' She was known also as Buí (or Boí), and under this name she is described as the wife of the god Lugh, who is elsewhere represented as a model of kingship, and she is brought into a close association with the megalithic monument of Knowth in Co. Meath.

In the eighth or ninth century one of the monastic *literati,* availing himself of a semantic ambiguity in the word *caillech,* invented the fiction that she had taken the nun's veil *(caille)* in the end of her days. He went on to compose around this notion a poem as rich in its symbolism as in its lyric beauty, in which the 'Nun' of Bérre contrasts her present state of penury and physical decay with other glorious days when she was the companion of princes:

Swift chariots
and horses that carried off the prize,
once I had plenty of them:
a blessing on the King who granted
  them.

My body seeks to make its way
to the house of judgement;
when the Son of God thinks it time,
let him come to claim his loan.

My arms when they are seen
are bony and thin;
dear was the craft they practised,
they would be around glorious
  kings . . .

I envy nothing that is old
except the Plain of Femhen;
though I have donned the thatch of
  age,
Femhen's crown is still yellow.

The Stone of the Kings in Femhen,
Rónán's Fort in Breghon,
it is long since storms first reached
  them,
but their cheeks are not old and
  withered . . .

I have had my day with kings,
drinking mead and wine;
today I drink whey and water
among shrivelled old hags . . .

The flood-wave,
and the swift ebb;
what the flood brings you
the ebb carries from your hand . . .

Happy is the island of the great sea,
for the flood comes to it after the
  ebb;
as for me, I do not expect
flood after ebb to come to me.

The real subject of this poem, 'the greatest of Irish poems' it has been claimed, is the deep incompatibility between Christianity and the world of pagan belief and the inevitable outcome of their conflict in the conquest and impoverishment of the latter. It is one of the great crucial themes of the Irish past and it is handled here with an artistic restraint and a depth of understanding and compassion that match its importance. In the present context, however, the significant thing is that the monastic poet should have chosen to present this great ideological theme through the legend of the Caillech Bhérri, mother-goddess, shaper and guardian of the land . . . and consort of kings.

The same kind of functional and aspectual variation holds true for Brighid. The composite legend of goddess and saint connects her on the one hand with learning, craftsmanship and healing and on the other with childbirth and animal abundance – all of them predominantly pacific concerns. Yet in time of war St Brighid was wont to intervene in favour of the Leinstermen and more

Hoard of gold objects from Broighter, Limavady, Co. Derry. Included are a model boat, complete with stepped mast, oars, steering oar, etc., a small hanging bowl, a large hollow collar (see page 74), two necklets of twisted gold and two necklets of fine chain. National Museum of Ireland, Dublin.

or less in the manner of the pagan war-goddess. But there is no essential inconsistency here, for Brighid was tutelary goddess of the land of Leinster and, as such, she was as much concerned with its political as with its economic well-being. In this, the interests of the territorial goddess coincide with those of the sacral kingship: the criterion of a rightful king is that the land should be prosperous and inviolate under his rule – and this can be achieved only if he is accepted as her legitimate spouse by the goddess who personifies his kingdom.

The Heroic Tradition

The Ulster Cycle

Irish literature knows many heroes and many tales cast in the heroic mould, but it has only one clearly defined Heroic Age. This is assigned by learned tradition to a period about the birth of Christ and it concerns primarily the Ulaidh, who were once the dominant people in Ulster and from whom that province takes its name. The earliest written record of this tradition belongs to the seventh century, but there can be no doubt that it had already behind it several centuries of oral existence. It pictures an aristocratic warrior-society with a La Tène culture, which in Ireland – secure as she was from Roman civilisation – survived more or less intact until after the establishment of Christianity. The social conditions described in the Ulster cycle show many striking correspondences with those reported of independent Gaul.

During this heroic age the Ulaidh were ruled by Conchobhar mac Nessa, who had his royal court at Emhain Mhacha near the present city of Armagh. He was the focus of a society of heroes of whom the most celebrated, after Cú Chulainn, were Conall Cernach and Ferghus mac Roich. Other prominent members of this heroic company were the druid Cathbhadh, who sometimes took precedence over the king himself, the wise Sencha mac Ailella, 'pacifier of the Ulster warriors', who quelled dissension and combat by his gentle intervention, and Bricriu *Nemhthenga*, 'Poison-tongue', the inveterate mischief-maker of the cycle who was as eager to incite strife as was Sencha to allay it.

The primary concern of heroic literature is with heroic action, and in this the Ulster cycle runs true to type. Tribal warfare and individual prowess are its constant preoccupation, and its principal saga tells of a great conflict between the Ulstermen on the one hand and, on the other, Medhbh and the Connachtmen supported by the rest of Ireland. The object of Medhbh's drive against Ulster was to seize possession of the great bull of Cuailnge, which, as we have seen, was of divine origin. But in this hour of danger the Ulstermen were prostrated by the strange illness to which they had been subjected by Macha's curse, and for as long as their debility lasted, the defence of the province was maintained single-handed by the youthful Cú Chulainn. By engaging in a long series of single combats with heroes of the opposing army, Cú Chulainn contrived to hinder the Connacht advance until the men of Ulster recovered their strength. They then attacked and routed the Connacht forces in a mighty battle. The Brown Bull of Cuailnge had already been captured by the Connachtmen and was now taken with them on their retreat, and the tale ends with the tremendous encounter in which the bull of Cuailnge defeated and slew the Finnbhennach, the 'white-horned' bull of Connacht, before itself expiring from its great exertion.

The Foretales: Deirdre and the Sons of Uisnech

However, *Táin Bó Cuailnge* is only one, albeit the most important, of a numerous cycle of tales. Some of these are designated 'foretales' *(remhscéla)* and are in one sense or another prefatory to the main saga, but the majority are independent accounts of the deeds of the Ulstermen. Of the 'foretales' several purport to describe how Ailill and

Left and below. Bronze shield with glass inlay, perhaps of the second century B.C., from the River Witham near Lincoln. It is a long Celtic shield of the kind which appears for example on the Gundestrup cauldron (see page 28). It has a central spine with a central boss and two terminal ornamented discs. Around the central boss there is the faint outline of a stylised boar which was formerly fixed to the shield with rivets. British Museum, London.

Medhbh contrived to win allies for their expedition against Ulster and to obtain cattle for the provisioning of their army during the campaign. Another, 'The Revelation of *Táin Bó Cuailnge*', concerns the history and provenance of the saga: by the seventh century, we are told, it had been largely forgotten and was only recovered when the *filidh*, having recourse to an enforcement procedure familiar to Irish and Indian law, fasted against Ferghus mac Roich until the ancient hero arose from his grave and related the mighty deeds of which he himself had been witness. Yet another, *Longes mac nUisnigh*, 'The Exile of the Sons of Uisnech', explains the strange circumstance that Ferghus and a number of other Ulster heroes are found, not among their fellow-Ulstermen, but in the entourage of Ailill and Medhbh during the events of *Táin Bó Cuailnge*. This explanation serves to anchor the tale within the context of the war between Ulster and Connacht, but otherwise it is rather peripheral to the theme of the tale: essentially, and notwithstanding its title, this story is

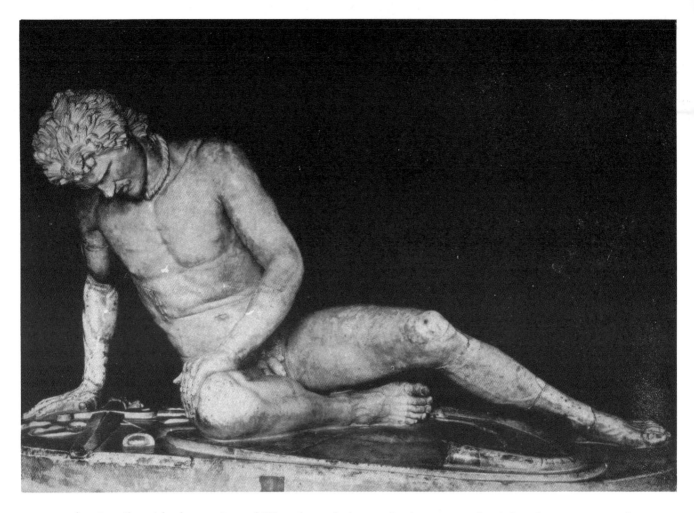

concerned primarily with the tragic fate of Deirdre.

Before Deirdre's birth it was prophesied by Cathbhadh the druid that she would be a woman of incomparable beauty but that she would also be the cause of much violence and suffering among the Ulstermen. Some thought that the child should be killed, but King Conchobhar ordered that she be brought up in seclusion until such time as he might take her for his wife. And so she was reared in a place apart until 'she was by far the most beautiful girl who had ever been in Ireland'. One day as she watched her foster-father flaying a calf on the snow in winter, she saw a raven drinking the blood on the snow, and she said to Lebhorcham, the wise woman who was her companion: 'Lovable would be the man on whom would be those three colours: his hair like the raven, his cheek like the blood, and his body like the snow.' And Lebhorcham told her that there was such a man, namely Naoise son

of Uisnech, and she resolved to see him. Once as he chanced to pass near by, she contrived to meet him on the road. 'Fair is the heifer that goes past me', said Naoise. 'Heifers are wont to be big,' she said, 'where there are no bulls.' 'You have the bull of the province', said he, 'the king of the Ulaidh.' 'I would choose between the two of you', said Deirdre, 'and I would take a young bull like you.' But Naoise was conscious of Cathbhadh's prophecy and would not be moved until Deirdre threatened him with shame and derision if he refused to take her with him. In this way she involved his personal honour – the supreme consideration to the heroic conscience – and compelled him to violate the bonds of obligation and loyalty to his king.

Together with his brothers Ardán and Ainnle he eloped with Deirdre and the tale subsequently tells of their precarious existence in Ireland and Scotland, harassed by Conchobhar and imperilled by the fatal attraction

of Deirdre's beauty. In time, however, the Ulstermen relented and persuaded Conchobhar to invite the Sons of Uisnech home and to send Ferghus mac Roich as surety for their safe conduct. But the shadow of Cathbhadh's prophecy still hung over them, and when they finally arrived at Emhain Mhacha Naoise and his brothers were treacherously slain and Deirdre taken by Conchobhar. Enraged by this violation of his word Ferghus wrought havoc at Emhain before taking his followers to the court of Ailill and Medhbh of Connacht.

For a year Deirdre was with Conchobhar, mourning and cherishing the memory of Naoise and his brothers. And once when Conchobhar asked her what she most hated, she replied 'You and Eoghan mac Durthacht', for it was Eoghan who had murdered Naoise. 'You shall be a year with Eoghan then', replied Conchobhar. But next day as she travelled with them both to the assembly of Macha – 'like a sheep between two

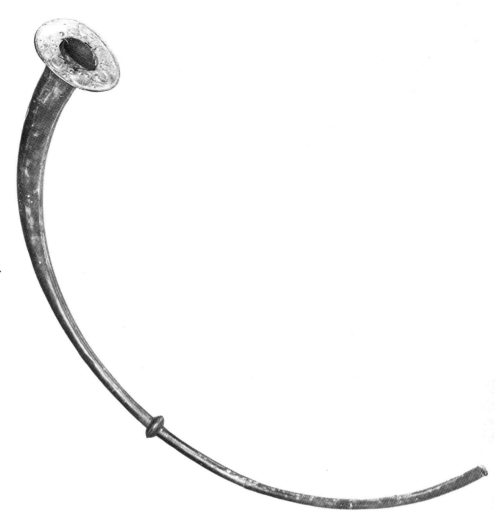

Right. Bronze horn with ornamental disc at the bell mouth, from Loughnashade, Navan townland, Co. Armagh. It may have been used for ceremonial purposes. National Museum of Ireland, Dublin.

Opposite. The 'Dying Gaul'. A Roman marble copy of the bronze statue erected by Attalos I of Pergamon in the third century B.C. after his triumph over the Galatians of Asia Minor. The warrior is naked but for a torc about his neck and thus illustrates vividly the testimony of classical authors that the Celts went into battle naked, carrying only their weapons. Museo Capitolino, Rome.

rams' jested Conchobhar — she cast herself from the chariot and shattered her head against a stone. This was the tragic death of Deirdre and the Sons of Uisnech.

The theme of this story is a familiar one in Celtic literature: the categories of tales cultivated by the *filidh* included one known as *aitheda,* 'elopements', and in most of these a youthful and vigorous lover is opposed to a mature and possessive husband. In addition *Longes mac nUisnigh* embodies a mythological motif that is well attested both in literature and iconography, namely the union of a divine heroine with one of a closely bound trio of brothers. It does not necessarily follow, of course, that Deirdre herself was divine, and indeed the lack of placenames and of diffused traditions connected with her argues otherwise. But whether or not the literary character has a mythological past, the thematic content of her story and her dominant personality indicate clearly enough that she was conceived in the image of the divine *femme fatale* of Irish tradition.

The Feast of Bricriu

Of the many Ulster tales not specifically related to *Táin Bó Cuailnge* one of the most important is *Fledh Bhricrenn,* 'The Feast of Bricriu'. As the title suggests, the setting for this story, as for so many others in Irish literature, is the communal feast, an occasion of primary importance in all heroic societies. The prime mover here is Bricriu the trouble-maker, the Irish counterpart of the Scandinavian Loki. He invites the Ulstermen to a great feast which has taken a year to prepare, but they are very willing, indeed anxious, to forgo the honour, knowing full well his propensity for setting his guests by the ears. He will not be put off, however, and promises stern retribution if they refuse: 'I will stir up strife among the kings, leaders, heroes and lesser nobles, till they will slay one another . . . I will cause enmity beneath father and son so that they will kill each other. But if that be not possible, I will set mother and daughter at variance. And if that be not possible, I will cause strife between the two breasts of every woman in Ulster so that they will smite each other till they rot and putrefy.' In the face of such a threat the Ulstermen cannot but acquiesce.

The next episode turns upon the notion of the *curadhmhír,* the 'champion's portion', in other words the choicest joint of meat which was by tradition assigned at a feast to the supreme hero present. The antiquity of this custom among the Celts is evidenced by Posidonius who writes in the first century B.C. that *in former times* it was usual for the bravest hero at a feast to take the thigh piece, and if any other laid claim to it then they arose and engaged in single combat to the death. Another Ulster tale, the rumbustious and witty *Scéla Mucce Maic Da Thó,* 'The Story of Mac Da Thó's Pig', is entirely constructed around this motif. Mac Da Thó, who no doubt is really the god who presides over the otherworld feast, acts as host to the companies of Connacht and Ulster and provides a prodigious pig for their regalement. The problem then is to decide whose privilege it will be to carve the pig (and naturally to favour himself and his fellows with the greater part). Contenders are thick on the ground and heroic boasts and counter-boasts fly fast and furious until Conall Cernach makes his entry and silences the opposition with incontrovertible evidence of his primacy: the head of Connacht's most vaunted warrior at his belt. In

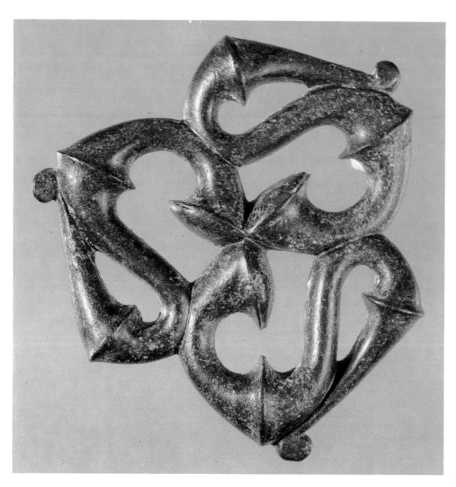

the event, however, his carving fails to satisfy the touchy Connachtmen and the dispute finally explodes into a pitched battle.

Bricriu is quick to seize the opportunity presented by this heroic etiquette. He goes first to Loeghaire *Buadhach,* 'The Triumphant', then to Conall Cernach and finally to Cú Chulainn, and persuades each of them in turn to claim the 'champion's portion' as his rightful privilege. The outcome, inevitably, is that the three heroes come to blows and the house becomes a seething tumult until Sencha intervenes to restore a temporary peace. It is decided to submit the dispute to the arbitration of Ailill of Connacht. But Bricriu has a second string to his bow. Seeing the wives of the three heroes leave the banqueting hall, he takes each of them aside, waxes eloquent in praise of her excellence of person and character, and promises that she who enters the hall first will be queen over the women of Ulster. This has a highly comic sequel as the stately progress of the noble

ladies, each dissembling her true purpose, gradually degenerates into a frenzied scramble for precedence. And as Loeghaire and Conall tear down pillars of the house to allow their wives access, Cú Chulainn simply raises his side of the building from the ground so that his wife and her companions may walk in unimpeded.

Eventually the heroes proceed to Connacht where they are tested by a fearsome ordeal and the primacy is awarded to Cú Chulainn. But the verdict is challenged by Loeghaire and Conall on their return to Emhain and they are then sent to Cú Roí mac Dáiri in the south-west of Ireland. Here after further trial of their valour Cú Roi also adjudges the 'champion's portion' to Cú Chulainn, and again the other two deny the judgement once they reach Emhain. This stalemate is the prelude to what is doubtless the best-known episode in *Fledh Bhricrenn.* One evening as the Ulstermen were assembled at Emhain they beheld a huge and monstrously ugly churl or herdsman

(bachlach) enter the hall. He brought a singular challenge: he would allow one of their heroes to cut off his head on condition that they reverse roles on the following night. Loeghaire and Conall both accept and behead the giant, but when the time comes each shirks his own part of the bargain. Finally Cú Chulainn takes up the challenge and beheads the giant, who picks up his severed head and walks off. When he returns the next evening, Cú Chulainn places his neck on the block in readiness to receive the blow that is due, but the giant raises his mighty axe to the ridge-pole of the hall only to bring the blunt edge gently down upon his neck, saying: 'Rise up, Cú Chulainn. Vain is it for any warrior of Ulster or Ireland to seek to contend with you in bravery and prowess and truth. Henceforth, to you shall belong the primacy of the warriors of Ireland and the "champion's portion".' The giant challenger is really the protean Cú Roí mac Dáiri come to vindicate his previous judgement.

Cú Roí is himself one of the most intriguing figures among the Irish divinities. He is portrayed as a master of sorcery and a habitual traveller whose martial conquests extend throughout the lands of the earth: from the age of seven years, when he took up arms, until he died, he had not reddened his sword in Ireland nor had the food of Ireland passed his lips. Each night, in whatever part of the world he might be, he chanted a

magic spell so that his fortress in Kerry revolved as swiftly as a millstone and its entrance could never be found after sunset. In his guise of giant churl or herdsman he has a number of analogues or derivatives in the Arthurian cycle, and indeed the whole episode of the beheading test evidently passed from Ireland to Wales and thence to continental Europe, to become part of several French and German romances as well as the Middle English poem *Sir Gawain and the Green Knight*. He evokes comparison with Pushan, the Indian cowherd deity who surveys the universe, protects cattle, acts as guide to the otherworld and aids in the revolution of day and night.

We have seen that in the story of Bricriu's Feast Cú Roí exalts Cú Chulainn, but there is another tale in which on the contrary he utterly humiliates him. On a raid upon the otherworld, here located in Scotland, Cú Chulainn and the Ulstermen encounter an uncouth-looking stranger who turns out to be Cú Roí and to whom they promise first choice of the booty in return for his help in storming the enemy stronghold. Largely through his might and prowess they succeed in carrying off the girl *Bláthnad*, 'Little Flower', together with a magic cauldron of plenty and three marvellous cows, but when it comes to the point they refuse to honour their promise to him. However, in no

way disconcerted, Cú Roí seizes cows, cauldron and woman and, stowing them in various parts of his huge person takes his leave. Of the Ulstermen only Cú Chulainn attempts to hinder his departure and Cú Roí simply takes hold of him, thrusts him into the earth to his armpits and – final ignominy – shaves off his hair with his sword. Afterwards Cú Chulainn hides himself away from the Ulstermen for a year. Then, at the time of Samhain, he makes a tryst with Bláthnad, and she, like her near-namesake Blodeuwedd in Welsh, betrays her husband so that he is taken unawares by the Ulstermen and slain. But even then Cú Roí does not go unavenged: his poet

Fercherdne, seeing Bláthnad standing close to the edge of the sheer cliff, rushes forward and, clasping his arms about her, plunges them both to their deaths on the strand below.

Cú Chulainn

Cú Chulainn's ungentle chastening by Cú Roí is not so much a depreciation of the hero as it is a manifestation of the deity's incomparable might. In the company of mortal heroes Cú Chulainn has no peer, and the part assigned to him in the *Táin* reflects faithfully enough his role throughout the cycle: he is the invincible hero to whom fate ordains a short life with lasting glory. His birthtale *(combert)* makes him son of the god Lugh and of Deichtine, daughter – or sister – of King Conchobhar, but it was also believed that Conchobhar himself begot him upon Deichtine. He was thus distinguished by a combination of two features which frequently mark the sacred birth of the hero: incest and procreation by a god. Another such feature is the motif of the congenital animals: certain

animals are born at the same time as the hero – in the case of the Welsh Pryderi it is a foal, in that of Cú Chulainn twin foals which later became his famed horses, the Grey of Macha and the Black of Saingliu.

The 'Boyhood Deeds' *(Macghnímhartha)* of Cú Chulainn constitute a separate narrative within the context of *Táin Bó Cuailnge*. His period of initiation into the heroic life begins when he makes his way alone to Emhain Mhacha and routs the

---

Above. A relief of severed heads which once adorned a pillar at the Celto-Ligurian temple of Entremont (Bouches-du-Rhône), second century B.C. Musée Granet, Aix-en-Provence.

Opposite. Portico of the Celto-Ligurian temple of Roquepertuse (Bouches-du-Rhône), belonging to the third or fourth century B.C. Its three pillars are furnished with niches for human skulls and on the lintel stands a great bird rather like a goose. Classical writers bear witness to the veneration of the human head among the Celts and especially to their practice of taking the heads of their slain enemies and preserving them as trophies. This is abundantly confirmed by the insular

literature, for example in 'The Story of Mac Da Thó's Pig', as well as by the archaeological evidence.

But the literature also treats the severed head, not as a mere trophy in the purely heroic ambiance, but as the source of a sacred and generally beneficient energy, and as such the object of profound respect and reverence. Basically it seems to have functioned as a symbol of the divine and the supernatural, a source of prosperity and fertility, and an apotropaic instrument to ward off evil from the individual and from the community as a whole. It is, for example, frequently associated in the literature, as in the archaeology, with the sacred waters of springs and lakes and rivers, traditional sources of healing and fertility, and is credited with a motive efficacy independent of the body as a whole (see for example the illustrations on pages 7, 32 left, 41 right and 60). The head of Bendigeidfran presided over the otherworld and protected the kingdom of Britain after its burial, and, if Dr Máire MacNeill is right, the deity represented by the three-faced head of Corleck may have extended his protective and propitious gaze out over the ripening corn-fields from the summit of Corleck Hill in Co. Cavan. The veneration of the head is not peculiar to the Celts, but they made of it an essential element of their ideology, to such a degree that it became, in Dr Anne Ross's words, 'the most typical Celtic religious symbol'. Musée Borély, Marseilles.

thrice fifty youths reared there under Conchobhar's protection. Then follows an episode in which his new status is marked by a change of name. When he is attacked by the savage hound that guards the land of Culann the smith, he hurls the ball he has been playing with down its gaping throat and, seizing the animal with his bare hands, dashes it to pieces against a pillar-stone. Culann complains bitterly of his loss and the boy undertakes to perform the hound's function for as long as may be necessary. It is from this circumstance that he is henceforth named Cú Chulainn, 'The Hound of Culann', for until this time he was known as *Sédanta*. The next stage in his initiation is the taking of arms. Learning from Cathbhadh the druid that whoever takes up arms on this particular day will be famous forever, though short-lived, he goes immediately to seek arms of Conchobhar, saying: 'Provided that my fame lives, I care not if I be on this earth but a single day.' He breaks fifteen sets of weapons that are offered to him before he is finally given those of the king.

Thus equipped he sets out upon his first warlike exploit. Ranging in his chariot beyond the southern boundaries of Ulster, he seeks out and slays the three fearsome sons of Nechta Scéne, who have slaughtered as many Ulstermen as remain alive. On the way back he captures a great stag and shoots down a flock of swans without killing them, and it is thus he approaches Emhain Mhacha in the heat of his battle frenzy, with the stag running behind the chariot, the tethered swans flying above it and the severed heads of the sons of Nechta Scéne within. To ward off his fury, which does not discriminate between friend and foe, the Ulsterwomen, led by Mughain their queen, go forth naked to meet him. He hides his face in confusion and is immediately seized by the warriors and plunged successively into three vats of cold water. The first bursts asunder, the second seethes with great bubbles, and the third becomes warm. When he has been restored by this treatment to a state of reason, he is clothed by the queen in

a blue cloak and admitted – a fledged hero – to the royal household.

The incidents in this sequence reflect substantially the scenario of heroic initiation as it is found throughout the world, though some details in it are more specifically Indo-European. Dumézil has suggested that the fight with the three sons of Nechta belongs to a recurrent Indo-European theme of the hero's encounter with a trio of adversaries or with a three-headed monster. The intervention of the women has analogies in Celtic and other traditions and is evidently a ritual act here employed as a means of propitiation. The concept of the hero as one who is *fired* with an ardent fury belongs to a wide-spread notion that sacred power is marked by an intense accession of physical heat. Thus the hero's battle ardour is essentially a magico-religious experience signalling his entry into the warrior class and his capacity to discharge its corporate function. In Cú Chulainn's case it is accompanied by a temporary physical distortion *(riastradh)*: his body revolves within his skin, his hair stands up stiff with as it were a spark of fire on the tip of every strand, one eye becomes as small as the eye of a needle and the other monstrously large, his mouth is distended as far as his ears, and the 'warrior's light' arises from the crown of his head. By this startling transformation is his surge of martial vigour made manifest.

At a later stage Cú Chulainn goes abroad to be trained by the supernatural Scáthach and from her he acquires the warlike stratagems which render him invincible. During this same expedition he encounters the Amazonian Aífe and begets a son upon her. This son is Conlaí who later lands in Ulster, refuses to reveal his name when challenged, and is slain by his father, as Sohrab was slain by Rustum or Hadubrand by Hildebrand; evidently we have to do here with an old Indo-European mytho-heroic theme.

The heroic quality of Cú Chulainn's life is matched by the manner of his death. As so often in Irish

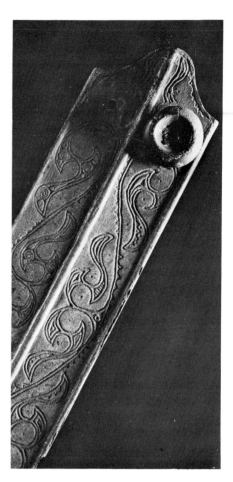

Above. A scabbard from a hoard at Lisnacroghera, Co Antrim. British Museum, London.

Opposite. Modern statue of the dying Cú Chulainn in the General Post Office, Dublin (Oliver Sheppard R.H.A. 1864-1941).

literature the tragic finale is clearly foreshadowed in preceding events, so that a sense of inescapable doom hangs over the whole narrative. In common with kings and with other heroic figures, Cú Chulainn is subject to a series of absolute prohibitions *(geissi* or *gessa)* whose violation involves certain disaster. Yet he now finds himself so placed that he is compelled to infringe these prohibitions one by one, and in the end he is overcome, not by the martial power of his enemies, but by their magic and treachery. Grievously wounded, he binds himself to a pillar-stone so that he may die standing, and it is only when the Morríghan and her sisters alight upon his shoulder in the form of hooded crows that his attackers dare to approach and to behead him.

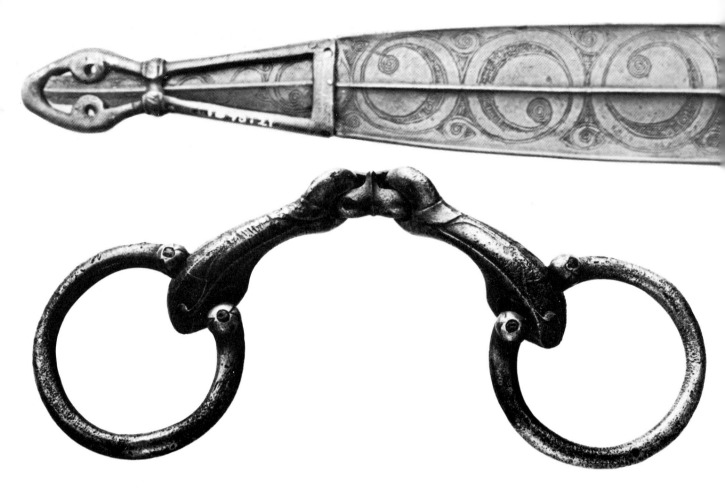

The Fionn Cycle

Here we enter upon another world to that of the Ulster tales. It is still a world of heroes, but one formed in a different mould and conditioned by a different temper of thought. The stories of Fionn mac Cumhaill and his companions seem always to have enjoyed popular favour and they remained prominent in the repertoire of Gaelic storytellers even to our own time. One of the commonest folk-names given to the dolmens which dot the Irish countryside is 'The Bed of Diarmaid and Gráinne', a striking testimony to the popularity of the tale which tells how Gráinne, Fionn's betrothed, eloped with Diarmaid ua Duibhne of the 'love-spot'. But, unlike the Ulster tales, they received scant recognition in the manuscript tradition until the twelfth century, after which they progressively displaced the Ulster cycle from its pre-eminent position. This fact may help to explain the mood of retrospection which characterises the cycle: its most important single composition, the

twelfth-century frame-story of *Agallamh na Seanórach* ('The Colloquy of the Old Men') is a nostalgic *recherche du temps perdu* based upon the fiction that Oisín, the son of Fionn, and Caoilte son of Rónán survived into the Christian period, met St Patrick and accompanied him over a large part of Ireland, recounting to him their numberless adventures of old as they were called to mind by the natural landmarks of the countryside. Its mood of nostalgic recollection of past glories dominates the subsequent literature of the cycle, and to this day a common expression in the Irish language for one who has outlived his contemporaries is *Oisín i ndiaidh na Féinne*, 'Oisín after the Fian'.

Fionn and his followers were known as the Fian and each individual member as a *féinnidh*; their adventures were *fianaigheacht* or *fian*-lore. In the beginning, however, the word *fian* was a common noun denoting a roving band of professional warriors, and, in point of fact,

the literature mentions several other *fiana* besides, but these were evidently eclipsed at an early period by the fame of Fionn's troop. They were bodies of warriors subject only to the authority of their own leaders and standing apart from and largely independent of normal society, but they were recognised by law and tradition as fulfilling a legitimate, even perhaps an essential, function. Many of the legends represent them as the defenders of the sovereignty of Ireland against external enemies, both natural and supernatural, and while these no doubt embody reminiscences of the historical struggles with the Viking invaders of the ninth century, nevertheless the underlying notion of Fionn and the Fian as protectors of the land seems to be much older.

Membership of the Fian was highly exclusive, but not hereditary: it could be acquired only by fulfilling certain conditions of admission and by undergoing initiatory ordeals as proof of exceptional dexterity and prowess. The would-be *féinnidh* was armed

with a shield and a hazel stick and placed standing up to his waist in a hole in the ground, and nine warriors cast their spears at him simultaneously. If he suffered hurt thereby he was not accepted into the Fian. Next his hair was braided and he was made to run through the woods of Ireland pursued at a brief interval by all the warriors. If he was overtaken and wounded he was not accepted. Moreover, if his weapons had quivered in his hand, if his hair had been disturbed by a hanging branch, or if a dead branch had cracked under his foot, then neither was he accepted. He had also to leap over a bough as high as his forehead while in full flight and pass under one as low as his knee, and he must be able to draw a thorn from his foot without slackening pace. Otherwise he was not admitted among the followers of Fionn.

The members of the Fian were hunters as well as fighters and this lends their adventures a greater mobility and freedom than is found in the Ulster tales. They move throughout the length and breadth of Ireland – and into Gaelic Scotland – in pursuit of their quarry, delighting in the exhilaration of the chase and in the endless variety of their natural surroundings. In retrospect, it seems almost inevitable that their legends should have assimilated the genre of lyrical nature poetry that had grown up in Irish from about the ninth century – as in these lines spoken by Caoilte in praise of the isle of Arran off the coast of Scotland:

Arran of the many stags,
the sea laps against its shoulder;
island where companies are
*   nourished,*

ridge on which blue spears are
*   reddened.*

Skittish deer upon its peaks,
tender bilberries upon its thickets;
cool water in its rivers,
mast upon its brown oaks...

Gleaning of purple upon its rocks,
faultless grass upon its slopes,
a mossy cloak upon its crags,
gambolling fawns, trout leaping...

Delightful it is when fair weather
*   comes:*
trout under the banks of its rivers;
seagulls answer each other round its
*   white cliff;*
delightful at all times is Arran.

This affinity with untamed nature and with the world beyond the bounds of organised society is epitomised in an episode from *Agallamh na Seanórach*. Swift-footed Caoilte tells the Christian nobles of a later age of the division that was made of Ireland by the two sons of King Feradhach Fechtnach after their father's

Above. Bronze scabbard plate from a crannog at Lisnacroghera, Co. Antrim, perhaps second century B.C. The chape is cast in the shape of a stylised serpent's head. National Museum of Ireland, Dublin.

Left. Reverse of denarius of L. Cosconius. A warrior standing in his chariot hurls a spear while the horses are at full gallop. Normally, however, as in Irish literary tradition, the warrior would have been accompanied by his charioteer. Ashmolean Museum, Oxford.

Opposite. Decorated bronze three-link bridle-bit. Find-place not recorded. National Museum of Ireland, Dublin.

Below. A stone pillar decorated with human heads at the Celto-Ligurian temple of Entremont (Bouches-du-Rhône). Musée Granet, Aix-en-Provence.

death. One of them took her wealth and treasure, her herds of cattle, her settled dwellings and her fortresses, the other her cliffs and her estuaries, the fruits of her woods and of the sea, her salmon and her game. His listeners protest that this was no equitable division and that the former son had much the better part, to which Caoilte replied that the portion which they disparaged was the one he and his companions preferred.

Their freedom of movement is not confined to the actual land of Ireland, for one of the characteristics of their legend is the ease with which they pass from the natural world to the supernatural. Time after time they find themselves in pursuit of a magic stag or boar which leads them to a secluded dwelling where they encounter strange beings and undergo equally strange and often perilous experiences. In other ways too they maintain constant dialogue with the people of the *sidh* or subterranean otherworld. It is almost as if, living as they did outside the areas of organised society, they thereby enjoyed a closer sympathy with the supernatural and freer access to it. Certainly the stories of the Fian are more akin to the mythological tales than are those of the Ulster cycle. Whereas the latter have preserved the heroic, quasi-historical tradition of the Celts, the Fionn cycle belongs rather to that romantic-mythological tradition which eventually became part of European literature through the medium of Arthurian romance.

Fionn himself was both seer and poet (as we have seen, these were but two aspects of the same function). According to some tales he acquired the gift of prophecy and supernatural knowledge by tasting of the otherworld liquor, but the commonest belief was that whenever he sought clairvoyance he had merely to chew his thumb, for with it he had once touched the Salmon of Wisdom which he was cooking for his master in poetic learning and magic. It is also said that he took up the craft of poetry as a protection against his hereditary enemies of the House of Morna (for the professional poet

enjoyed a quasi-sacred immunity in early Irish society). This detail is found in the story of Fionn's birth and youthful deeds, versions of which have remained popular with unlettered storytellers till our own day (and which, incidentally, was one of the ultimate sources of Perceval's boyhood in *Le Conte del Graal* by the twelfth-century Chrétien de Troyes).

Fionn's father was slain by the Sons of Morna before he was born, and he was reared secretly in the forest by two women-warriors. But, in keeping with the normal pattern of the youth of a hero, Fionn soon showed his mettle in a series of precocious exploits which mark his initiation into the warrior confraternity. Thus he was only in his eighth year when he performed the feat which won him the headship of the Fian. On coming to Tara for the first time the boy found the whole company anxiously awaiting the arrival of a malevolent being named Aillén mac Midhna who came each year at the feast of Samhain and burned down the royal court after lulling its defenders to sleep with magic music. Fionn, however, was able to resist the music by pressing the point of a magic spear against his forehead, and when Aillén approached breathing fire he drove him off and then beheaded him. This is one of several different tales which are evidently variants of a myth which pictured Fionn as the vanquisher of a supernatural one-eyed burner. Even within the Fian he has an arch-rival named *Goll* ('One-eyed') mac Morna, otherwise known as *Aodh* ('Fire').

There is here an obvious analogy with the myth of Lugh's defeat of Balar of the evil eye and this analogy may be more then mere coincidence. For in point of fact there are considerable grounds for believing that Fionn was himself divine. He is probably to be equated with Gwynn ap Nudd who appears in Welsh tradition as a 'magic warrior-huntsman' and leader of the otherworld folk. Moreover, the Celtic form *vindos*, 'white', which gives Irish *Fionn* and Welsh *Gwynn*, is attested in continental Europe in

Above. A hunting scene depicted on a pillar at the monastery of Clonmacnois, Co. Offaly. It is one of a number of instances in which the monastic sculptures appear to draw upon traditional themes.

Opposite above. Decorated stone outside the entrance to the Bronze Age tumulus of New Grange, Co. Meath. The complex of tumuli on this site, near the Boyne river, though pre-Celtic, was assimilated to Gaelic mythological tradition. This photograph was taken before the recent reconstruction of the entrance to the mound.

Opposite below. Bronze boar figurine from Hounslow, Middlesex, first century B.C. to first century A.D. The boar is a familiar feature both of Celtic iconography and of the insular literary tradition; as Anne Ross has observed, on this evidence it would seem to have been 'the cult animal *par excellence* of the Celts'. British Museum, London.

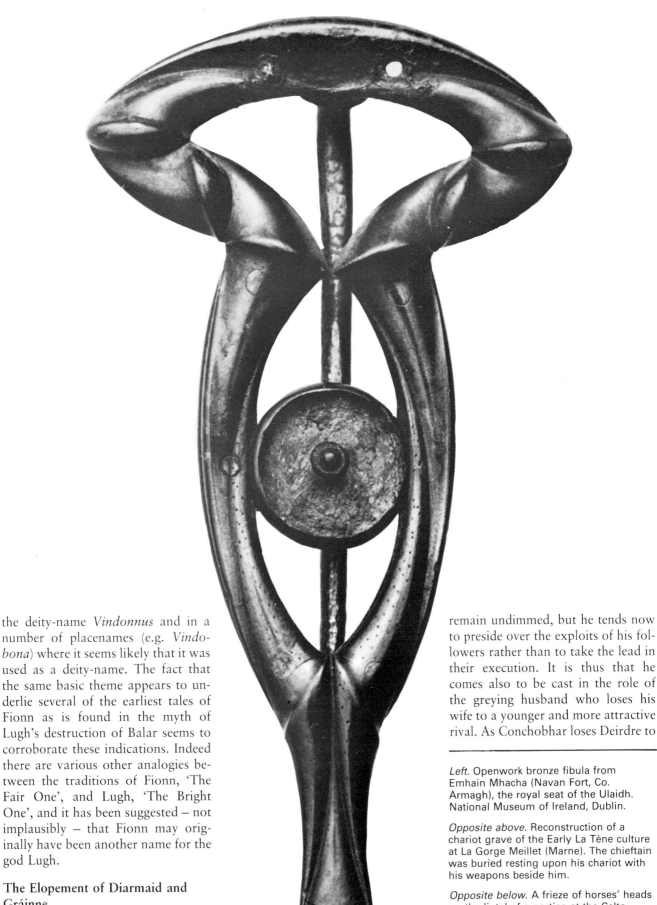

the deity-name *Vindonnus* and in a number of placenames (e.g. *Vindobona*) where it seems likely that it was used as a deity-name. The fact that the same basic theme appears to underlie several of the earliest tales of Fionn as is found in the myth of Lugh's destruction of Balar seems to corroborate these indications. Indeed there are various other analogies between the traditions of Fionn, 'The Fair One', and Lugh, 'The Bright One', and it has been suggested – not implausibly – that Fionn may originally have been another name for the god Lugh.

The Elopement of Diarmaid and Gráinne

Often, like his British counterpart Arthur, Fionn is represented as an aging leader attended by a group of younger lieutenants: his power and renown remain undimmed, but he tends now to preside over the exploits of his followers rather than to take the lead in their execution. It is thus that he comes also to be cast in the role of the greying husband who loses his wife to a younger and more attractive rival. As Conchobhar loses Deirdre to

Left. Openwork bronze fibula from Emhain Mhacha (Navan Fort, Co. Armagh), the royal seat of the Ulaidh. National Museum of Ireland, Dublin.

Opposite above. Reconstruction of a chariot grave of the Early La Tène culture at La Gorge Meillet (Marne). The chieftain was buried resting upon his chariot with his weapons beside him.

Opposite below. A frieze of horses' heads on the lintel of a portico at the Celto-Ligurian sanctuary of Roquepertuse (Bouches-du-Rhône), third century B.C. Horses were evidently associated with the cult of the deity honoured here. Musée Borély, Marseilles.

Naoise and Arthur loses Gwenhwyfar to Medrawd (or to Melwas), so does Fionn lose Gráinne to Diarmaid ua Duibhne, 'the master and charmer of women'. The tale is found only in a late text, but it is already mentioned as 'The Elopement of Gráinne with Diarmaid' in a tenth-century saga-list and was undoubtedly a proximate source of the famous romance of Tristan and Iseult. It tells of the betrothal of Gráinne to Fionn, who was at this time a widower. For Gráinne, however, it was no affair of the heart, and on the night of the wedding-feast she contrived to effect a more compatible union. First she administered a sleeping potion to all but a chosen few of the assembled company and then she laid Diarmaid under magic bonds (gessa) to elope with her. For Diar-maid the power of the gessa outweighed his reluctance to break faith with his leader and he brought her away with him.

They first took refuge in a wood in Connacht, and here Diarmaid cut a clearing with seven doors to it and within it he laid a bed of rushes and birch-tips for Gráinne. When Fionn and his men surrounded them, Diarmaid's foster-father, the god Oenghus, came to their aid and spirited Gráinne away under his cloak, while Diarmaid with supreme agility leaped clear over the heads of the besiegers. Thereafter they continued to wander through Connacht and Munster, and for a long time Diarmaid remained loyal to Fionn and wherever they slept he left uncooked meat as a sign of their continence. But one day as they walked some muddy water splashed upon Gráinne's leg and she taunted Diarmaid with the remark that the water was bolder than he. It was then he yielded to her persistence and they became lovers. Eventually, by the good offices of Oenghus peace was made between Fionn and Diarmaid, though in his heart Fionn still nursed hopes of vengeance.

The lovers settled down, Gráinne bore Diarmaid four sons and a daughter and they lived in happy prosperity until the fatal chase of the magic boar of Beann Ghulban in Co. Sligo. This boar had once been Diarmaid's foster-brother by whom it had been prophesied that he would fall. But though his doom had thus been clearly prefigured, Diarmaid joined Fionn and the Fian in the great hunt and was grievously wounded before he slew the quarry. Only one thing could now save him: a draught of water from the hands of Fionn, who had the gift of healing. Much against his will Fionn was prevailed upon to go for water, but as he returned he remembered his beloved Gráinne and let it flow through his fingers. Twice he did this, and the third time, when he brought the water, he found that Diarmaid was dead.

All three actors in this tale appear to be divine, at least in origin. Fionn we have seen to be almost certainly so, and in Gráinne's case her name seems to imply as much: meaning literally 'ugliness' or 'repulsiveness', it suggests that Gráinne was once known as the loathsome hag who is transfigured into a being of incomparable beauty through marriage to her pre-ordained partner (see page 119). Diarmaid is sometimes known as Diarmaid *Donn*, 'Brown, Dark', and sometimes as Diarmaid son of Donn, and there is a strong presumption that he was originally one with the god Donn who ruled over the Irish otherworld of the dead. But though it is reasonably clear that they were all three deities, one cannot with any confidence presume to interpret their story in terms of their mythological status, nor indeed can one entirely discount the possible effect of the distorting lens of literary creativity. It may be noted that one of the few surviving traditions of Fionn's British counterpart, Gwynn ap Nudd, assigns him the part of the lover rather than that of the husband and engages him in an everlasting fight for the hand of the heroine. The story has it that Creiddylad the daughter of

Opposite. A small cult chariot from Merida in Spain, showing a mounted warrior in pursuit of a boar, second to first century B.C. It recalls the common insular theme of the hunting of a supernatural boar, as for example in the story of Arthur's pursuit of the Twrch Trwyth, in the Welsh tale of '*Culhwch and Olwen*'. Here Arthur and his men also hunt on horseback, whereas in the Irish Fionn cycle the hunters normally accompany their hounds on foot. Musée des Antiquités Nationales, St Germain-en-Laye.

Below. Portal dolmen at Kilclooney, Co. Donegal. Dolmens consist of a single chamber formed by three or more upright stones and roofed by a single capstone. Originally each was covered by a mound

of earth. They are widely distributed throughout Ireland and were commonly known by the popular term 'Bed of Diarmaid and Gráinne', an allusion to the tale of Gráinne's elopement with Diarmaid ua Duibhne and their flight together from the vengeance of Fionn.

Bottom left. The Turoe Stone in Co. Galway, third to first century B.C. Standing 4 feet (1.2 m) high, this granite block is decorated with curvilinear La Tène style motifs arranged asymmetrically and carved in low relief. It was evidently a cult stone.

Bottom right. Benbulben (Beann Ghulban) in Co. Sligo, where Diarmaid ua Duibhne was slain by the magic boar of the mountain.

Lludd Llaw Ereint had been given to Gwythyr son of Gwreidawl, but before the marriage had been consummated she was abducted by Gwynn ap Nudd. However, Arthur intervened to restore peace between the disputants, and the terms of peace were that the maiden should remain in her father's house and that Gwynn and Gwythyr should fight for her every May-day until Doomsday; the victor then should have Creiddylad.

The story of Diarmaid and Gráinne has been compared with that of Adonis and Aphrodite and with the exaltation of adulterous love and the worship of the goddess which were associated with the cult of Krishna in India. The analogies are unmistakable, but not so their significance. For the present let it suffice to say that the *aithedha* or 'elopements' to which the tale of Diarmaid and Gráinne belongs seem to continue an ancient

theme concerning the rivalry of a younger and an older deity for possession of a goddess, and that at some stage in its development this theme assumed the character of a conflict between love and honour, a conflict which we find in the stories of Deirdre and Gráinne amongst others and one which was to receive its ultimate and classical statement in the romances of Lancelot and Guinevere and of Tristan and Iseult.

Fionn and Arthur

Fionn also reveals obvious similarities to the British hero Arthur. Both defend their countries against foreign enemies and overcome fearsome monsters. Both invade the otherworld and both are hunters: *Culhwch and Olwen*, in a narrative which has many analogues among the legends of the Fian, tells how Arthur and his followers hunted the Twrch Trwyth, a magic and venomous boar, through part of Ireland, south Wales and Cornwall. Both their legends circulated for centuries among the common people before they won acceptance – and the sanction of the written word – from the *literati*, and both in their time were acclaimed throughout Europe: the Arthurian cycle during the twelfth and later centuries and the Fionn cycle in the eighteenth century when Macpherson's fabrications made the legend of Ossian (the Irish Oisín) a fashionable cult in the courts and salons of continental Europe. There are many other striking parallels between the two cycles, and even the title of *dux bellorum* which Nennius in the ninth century applies to Arthur is a tolerable Latin equivalent of Fionn's title of *ríghfhéinnidh*, 'king-féinnidh'. It is indeed possible that Arthur was a British leader of the late fifth century, as some sources indicate, but even if he was, the traditions which gathered about his name belonged to the fund of insular mythology which gave rise to the legend of Fionn mac Cumhaill.

Sacral Kingship

In Gaul the institution of kingship was already in rapid process of dissolution in Caesar's time. But among the insular Celts it proved more enduring, and in Ireland and Scotland its decline coincided with that of the entire Gaelic social system, which finally foundered in the seventeenth century. Indeed, to the Irish mind kingship and the public weal were so intimately related as to be at times almost synonymous, and in the deep misery of the eighteenth century when the poets lamented their country's servitude to a foreign oppressor and wishfully prophesied the return of the old order, it was always in terms of the restoration of the native kingship that they envisaged the great liberation. Since the Irish nobility had already been destroyed or dispersed throughout the armies of Europe, it was to the exiled Stuarts that the poets turned – *faute de mieux* – for a symbol of their deliverance. In the circumstances of the time, it was a gesture almost entirely devoid of political reality, but it was delivered with much eloquence and, above all, with a profound sense of tradition, for in thus making Ireland's salvation conditional upon the accession of a rightful and acceptable king, they were acting as the faithful transmitters of an age-old and uninterrupted belief.

However, paradoxically as it may appear, the earliest recorded tradition, namely the Laws, knew no king of Ireland, but only the king of a *tuath* (the basic territorial unit) and the king of a province. The notion of a king of Ireland with actual powers over the whole country is attested commonly in the literature but nevertheless it seems to be relatively late and to have been propagated from

Above. Bronze sword hilt from Ballyshannon, Co. Donegal, first century B.C. Similar sword hilts cast in the form of a human figure are known from continental Europe and Britain and this example may well be an import. National Museum of Ireland, Dublin.

Opposite. Yew tankard covered with bronze sheeting, with cast bronze handle, first century A.D., from Trawsfynydd, Gwynedd. Merseyside County Museum, Liverpool.

the ninth century onwards by native historians and learned poets working in the interest of the great dynasty of the Uí Néill, the descendants of Niall of the Nine Hostages.

And yet it cannot be wholly a new creation. For one thing, the 'king of Ireland' was also known frequently as king of Tara, and there is no lack of evidence to show that Tara must have been a sacred site of kingship from

time immemorial. It was situated within the central province, *Midhe*, which was itself enclosed by the other four provinces of the pentarchy, thus forming a cosmographic schema which has parallels in Indian and other traditions. The very word for a province, *cóigedh*, literally 'a fifth', presupposes a transcendant unity at the heart of which stands Tara, and, as Alwyn and Brinley Rees have pointed out, the traditional accounts of the disposition of the court of Tara show that it was conceived as a replica of this cosmographic schema.

Tara was also the site of the famous *Feis Temhra*, 'The Feast of Tara', which was held in pagan times to confirm or legitimise the recently elected king and during which, it would seem, his ritual marriage to the realm was celebrated (the word *feis* means both 'feast' and 'to sleep, spend the night'): as the early triad has it, the Feast of Tara was one of the 'three things that hallow a king'. On the Hill of Tara stood the Stone of Fál, the 'stone penis' which cried out when it came in contact with the man destined to be king. Since *Fál* is commonly used as a poetic or learned synonym for 'Ireland', obviously the kingship myth attaching to the Stone of Fál had a universal reference. While it does not follow from this that the king of Tara in the pre-Christian era held political sway over the whole of Ireland – otherwise this would no doubt have been recognised in the Laws – it is clear that he enjoyed a special prestige by virtue of his position at the sacred focus of kingship.

Ideally kingship was heritable within a family group (the *derbh-fhine*) comprising four generations: all living members of this group were potential successors and it was from their number that the new king was elected. But Irish tradition also knows of more ritual modes of selection. The first comprises several ordeals to test the candidate's fitness: a royal chariot that actively rejected him who was unworthy; a royal mantle that proved too big for him; two stones, with but a hand's breadth between them, which opened wide to give passage to the chariot of him who was found acceptable; and finally, of course, the Stone of Fál which clearly 'voiced' its assent. The second mode of selection was known as the *tarbhfhess*, 'bull-feast, or bull-sleep': a bull was killed, and a man ate his fill of its flesh, drank its broth and then lay down to sleep, and after an incantation had been chanted over him by four druids he saw in his sleep whoever was destined to be king. Both these methods of selection are expressly associated with the kingship of Tara, and it may be that they represent rituals once performed at the central seat of kingship.

A general feature of sacral kingship is the tendency to insulate the person of the king against the perils of the profane world and to regulate his conduct down to the merest details. A striking instance of this in Irish usage is the series of magically binding prohibitions (*geissi*) to which he is subjected simply by virtue of his office. The particular significance of these *geissi* is in most instances obscure: some may allude to circumstances that have once proved harmful and are therefore to be avoided, while others might seem wholly arbitrary. Thus the king of Ulster is forbidden to take part in the horse-race of Ráith Lini, to listen to the birds of Lough Swilly when the sun sets, to taste the flesh of Dáire's bull, to go into Magh Cobha in March and to drink the water of Bó

Nemhidh (a river) between dawn and darkness. What is clear, however, is that they relate to his sacral status — as, for example, do the rather similar interdictions attaching to the office of the Roman Flamen Dialis — and whenever fate impels him to violate them this is a clear portent that his kingship, and indeed his life, is at an end. Whether it was ever the practice in certain circumstances to set a term to the king's reign by subjecting him to a ritual death such as is attested in other societies cannot be demonstrated beyond doubt, but several episodes in early narrative indicate it as a definite possibility.

The qualities of a rightful king (which in Irish are comprised under the term *fír flaithemhan*, literally 'truth of the ruler') are reflected in the condition of his kingdom. They ensure peace and equity, security of the kingdom's borders, and material prosperity: the trees bend low with the weight of their fruit, the rivers and the sea teem with abundance of fish, and the earth brings forth rich harvests. Conversely, a king who is blemished in his conduct and character or in his person will bring about corresponding privations: for this reason Bres was deposed, since he was completely lacking in the princely virtue of liberality, and Nuadhu was obliged to abdicate once he lost his arm in battle. Cautionary instances were numerous and familiar, such as that of the usurper Cairbre Caitchenn, during whose reign there used to be but one grain on each corn-stalk and one acorn on each oak, and the rivers were without fish and the cattle without milk. In Welsh the same notion is at the origin of the sudden desolation of Dyfed in the Welsh tale of *Manawydan,* and in the Grail legend it recurs still more explicitly in the waste land which results from the maiming of the Fisher King.

The sacral king is the spouse of his kingdom and his inauguration ceremony is known as *banais ríghi,* 'wedding-feast of kingship'; in other words he is then ritually united with the sovereignty of the territory over which he rules. This is why the Feast of Tara could not be convened and Eochaidh Airemh's kingship ratified until he had sought out Édaín to be his queen: otherwise he would have been the supreme paradox of a king without sovereignty. As queen of Connacht, the goddess Medhbh required that her husbands be 'without niggardliness, without jealousy and without fear', that is to say, they must possess the paramount attributes of a king. As Medhbh Lethdherg of Leinster, her other manifestation, she cohabited with nine kings of Ireland and of her was it said: 'Great indeed was the power and influence of that Medhbh over the men of Ireland, for she it was who would not permit a king in Tara unless he had her for his wife.' Mór of Munster was spouse to two provincial kings and 'she was sought after by the kings of Ireland'.

The wedding ritual of the *banais ríghi* evidently comprised two main elements, a libation offered by the bride to her partner and the coition. The Sovereignty of Ireland appears to Conn of the Hundred Battles seated on a crystal throne and with a vat of red liquor beside her from which she serves him (and his successors) with a drink in a golden goblet, and the same essential function is implied in the name of the goddess Medhbh, 'The Intoxicating One'. The sexual element is almost always present, whether explicitly or by implication, and one of the normal ways of reporting the inauguration of a king is to say that he was wedded to (literally 'slept with') his kingdom.

As a result of this union the person of the goddess is sometimes utterly transformed. Just as the land lies barren and desolate in the absence of its destined ruler and is quickly restored to life by his coming, so the goddess who personifies the kingdom often appears ugly, unkempt and destitute until united with her rightful lord, when suddenly she is changed into a woman of shining beauty. One such tale is told of Niall Noíghiallach. He and his four brothers go hunting, find themselves astray in the wilderness and stop to cook part of the game they have killed. Each in turn goes off to look for water and comes upon a well guarded by a hideous crone who will give water only in return for a kiss. Three of the five brothers refuse

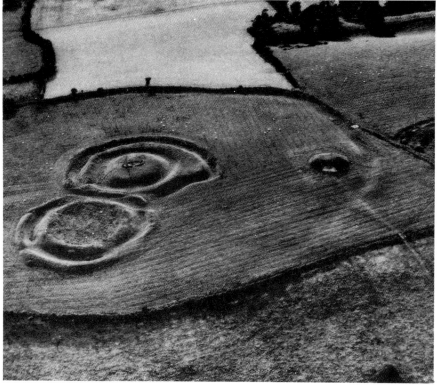

outright, Fiachra grants her a fleeting kiss, while Niall not merely kisses her but consents to lie with her too. Immediately she is transformed into a young girl more radiantly beautiful than the sun. She is, she explains, the sovereignty of Ireland and she foretells that Niall and his descendants will hold unbroken rule, apart from two kings of the posterity of Fiachra who were foretokened by his kiss.

This particular adaptation of the kingship myth is intended to account for the centuries-long hegemony of the Uí Néill, Niall's descendants, over the greater part of the country. It has a parallel in the Munster legend told of Lughaidh Laoighdhe, an ancestor of the pre-Goidelic people known as the Érainn and, almost certainly, an avatar of the god Lugh. Here the brothers' quarry is a magic fawn which is evidently another metamorphosis of the goddess: by

Left. Section of a cauldron from Rynkeby, Denmark, with a torc-bearing head, first century B.C. to first century A.D. The vessel may be of Gaulish manufacture. Nationalmuseet, Copenhagen.

Opposite below. Air photograph of the central earthworks on the Hill of Tara, Co. Meath. Though rising only some 300 feet (90 m) higher, the hill commands extensive views over the central plains of Ireland and this was no doubt one reason why it was chosen as a religious site and focus of the sacred kingship. The early literature describes a whole complex of buildings situated on or around the hill, and it was here stood the great *Tech Midhchuarta*, 'The Hall of Mead-circuit', described in terms of extravagant splendour in the *dinnshenchas* and in several of the sagas. Tara was the scene of the ritual marriage-feast, *Feis Temhra*, by which the status of a new king was confirmed and his union with his kingdom solemnised. This feast was last celebrated in the reign of Diarmaid mac Cerbhaill in the mid sixth century, and its discontinuance probably 'marks the final christianisation of the Tara monarchy'.

capturing it, as well as by sleeping with the hag, Lughaidh marks himself out as future king. This fawn of sovereignty is a forerunner of the magic stags which appear in the story of Perceval and in other Arthurian romances.

It need hardly be stressed that the sacral kingship and the sacred marriage of king and goddess are not peculiarly Celtic, the former being more or less universal and the latter well attested from India and the Near East. What is remarkable, however, is the persistence and vigour of these concepts in the tradition of the only Celtic society which remained relatively untouched by Roman civilisation (and that they were also present in British tradition is evident from their prominent role in the Arthurian legend). They profoundly influenced the telling and writing of Irish history and doubtless they contributed

much to its making. One may reasonably wonder, for instance, whether Boudica of the British Iceni or Cartimandua of the Brigantes would have figured so prominently in history but for the fact that the Celts venerated a sovereign and dominant goddess variously known as Medhbh, or Macha, or Brigantia.

And Irish kings were no less aware than their poet-propagandists of the action of myth on history. The ninth-century king of Munster, Feidhlimidh mac Crimthainn, had designs on the lordship of Ireland, and according to some Munster sources he did in fact achieve his aim. In A.D. 838, report the Annals of Innisfallen, he obtained the submission of Niall Caille, king of Tara, and two years later he raided northwards as far as Tara and seized Gormlaith, Niall's queen, together with her female retinue. It is hard to believe that Feidhlimidh did not have an eye to tradition when he thus abducted Queen Gormlaith from the sacred seat of kingship, for in the Irish context his action must surely have implied that just as he had taken possession of Niall's spouse of flesh and blood so also was he in virtual possession of that other spouse to

whom Niall laid claim, namely the sovereignty of Ireland.

The concept of the land of Ireland as a goddess was deeply rooted and it did not die easily. When the Gaels first set foot on its soil, so the legend tells us, they were met by the lady Ériu, queen and eponym of the island, and ages later when Gaelic society had been broken by plantation and by the sword, the poets of the seventeenth and eighteenth century still pictured their land as a woman languishing in yearning for her absent spouse, or even as a shameless prostitute granting her favours to the boorish foreigner who had usurped the place of her rightful partner. And finally from these Gaelic poets of the 'hidden Ireland' the concept was borrowed by various individual poets of Anglo-Ireland, and notably by the greatest among them, W. B. Yeats. The ring of tradition is clear and loud in the final words of his play, *Cathleen Ni Houlihan*, at that point where the mysterious old woman of the roads has just gone from the house: 'Did you see an old woman going down the path?' Peter Gillane asks his young son Patrick – and the answer is: 'I did not, but I saw a young girl, and she had the walk of a queen.'

The Otherworld

Nothing about the Celts is more certain than that they believed in a life after death. On this the testimonies of archaeology, classical commentary and insular tradition are essentially at one. The grave furniture which accompanies Celtic burials presupposes such a belief, classical authors make explicit statement of it, and insular storytellers have woven it imaginatively into the fabric of their literature.

That this belief was part of the formal teaching of the Gaulish druids is confirmed by virtually every classical author who has written of the Celts. Caesar, like the good pragmatist that he was, takes the consequence for the cause and assumes that the object of the druids in preaching the immortality of the soul was to ensure that their followers, through disregard of death, would be the more valorous in war. According to others, for Caesar is ambiguous on this point, the druids taught that the soul passed from one body to another, and this they relate specifically to the Pythagorean theory of metempsychosis, or transmigration of souls. The idea has an obvious attraction and it is still not infrequently echoed by modern writers on the druids, though the actual evidence for it is unconvincing. It is true that in Irish and Welsh literature shapeshifting is commonplace, and there are even a number of instances of characters undergoing a prolonged series of metamorphoses – mention has already been made of Fintan, sole survivor of the first invasion of Ireland, and of the swineherd antecedents of the divine bulls of *Táin Bó Cuailnge,* and Welsh tradition has a worthy parallel to these in the mythical Taliesin (as opposed to his historical counterpart), who by his

own boast had undergone countless transformations and was as old as the world's history – but this is something quite different to Pythagorean metempsychosis or to the *samsara* of Hindu belief. Far from implying that the process of serial reincarnation affected all animate beings, these legends restrict it to a relatively small number of instances, all of them concerning either deities or mythical personages. Assuming, however, that similar legends were current among the Gaulish Celts, it can be readily appreciated that they would have lent themselves to misinterpretation by classical commentators familiar with the Pythagorean theory.

But the classical sources also contain allusions to a different concept of immortality among the Celts. Lucan in his well-known apostrophe to the druids attributes to them the teaching that after death human souls continue to control their bodies in another world *(orbe alio)*, which is not the silent abode of Erebus or the deep and pallid realm of Dis. Therefore, he adds, the Celts accept death without trepidation since it is for them only a juncture in a long life. This otherworld of corporeal beings which Lucan contrasts with the gloomy classical underworld peopled by pale insubstantial shades evidently corresponds to the preternatural world which figures so largely in the traditions of the Irish and the Welsh.

This otherworld of the insular Celts is a changing scene of many phases, and if one's mind instantly conjures up an image of an Elysian land where men and women live in unending happiness, the explanation may well be that this particular image of the otherworld was handled repeatedly and with remarkable sensitivity by a

Right. Base-plate from the interior of the Gundestrup cauldron showing a warrior – or deity – apparently about to plunge his weapon into the neck of a prostrate bull. Some have ascribed this scene to Mithraic influence, while others have stressed the prominent role assigned to the bull in Celtic tradition. The accompanying dogs perhaps suggest a hunting theme, but there is no obvious pendant to this in extant insular Celtic narrative. Irish has the method of divination known as the *tarbhfhess*, 'bull-feast' (see page 117), with which one may compare Pliny's account of the ritual sacrifice of bulls by the Gaulish druids, but the setting scarcely seems compatible with that of the Gundestrup cauldron scene. Nationalmuseet, Copenhagen.

Below. Grianán Ailigh, Co. Donegal. This stone fort standing on the summit of an 800-foot (245-m) high hill was once the royal seat of the Northern Uí Néill.

succession of monastic lyric poets and storytellers from the seventh century onwards. Certain features recur continually in their descriptions of it. It is 'The Land of the Living', *Tír inna mBeo,* where sickness and decay are unknown. It is a land of primeval innocence where the pleasures of love are untainted by guilt. Its women are numerous and beautiful and they alone people some of its regions, so that then it becomes literally 'The Land of Women', *Tír inna mBan.* It is filled with enchanting music from bright-plumaged birds, from the swaying branches of the otherworld tree, from instruments which sound without being played and from the very stones. And it has abundance of exquisite food and drink, and magic vessels of inexhaustible plenty. The woman who comes to invite Bran mac Febhail on his wondrous voyage there pictures it first as an island, but later as 'three times fifty distant isles', far to the west of Ireland:

There is a distant isle
around which sea-horses glisten,
a fair course on which the white
*   wave surges,*
four pedestals uphold it.

A delight to the eye, a glorious
*   range,*
is the plain on which the hosts hold
*   games;*
coracle races against chariot
in the plain south of Findargad.

Pillars of white bronze beneath it
shining through aeons of beauty,

Left. Rectangular sandstone pillar from Steinebronn (Waldenbuch), Württemberg, of the fourth to third century B.C. The damaged upper portion, which evidently represented a human torso, now lacks its head, but the left forearm remains. The crude naturalism of this arm contrasts with the abstract ornament below: a band of rectilinear patterns above a panel of stylised curvilinear vegetal decoration. Württembergisches Landesmuseum, Stuttgart.

Opposite. Three mother-goddesses. Württembergisches Landesmuseum, Stuttgart.

lovely land through the ages of the
world,
on which the many blossoms fall.

Unknown is wailing or treachery
in the happy familiar land;
no sound there rough or harsh,
only sweet music striking on the ear.

Then if one sees the Silvery Land
on which dragonstones and crystals
rain,
the sea breaks the wave upon the
land
with crystal tresses from its mane. . .

The host races along Magh Mon,
a beautiful sport that is not feeble;
in the many-coloured land of
surpassing beauty
they expect neither decay nor death.

Another poem of the invitation-type
mentions briefly the paradisiac com-
munism of unending abundance and
exemplifies the sensuous use of colour
which marks early Irish lyric verse in
general and especially the descriptions of the blissful otherworld:

There, there is neither 'mine' nor
'thine';
white are teeth there, dark the
brows;
a delight of the eye the array of our
hosts;
every cheek there is of the hue of
the foxglove.

Purple the surface of every plain,
a marvel of beauty the blackbird's
eggs;
though the Plain of Fál be fair to
see,
'tis desolate once you have known
Magh Már.

Fine though you think the ale of
Ireland,
more exhilarating still is the ale of
Tír Már;
a wondrous land is the land I tell of,
youth does not give way to age
there.

Sweet warm streams flow through
the land,
the choice of mead and of wine;
splendid people without blemish,
conception without sin, without lust.

This world transcends the limita-
tions of human time; the mortal re-
turning from a visit there may
suddenly become aged and decrepit
on contact with the material world,
or may simply dissolve into dust. It
also transcends all spatial definition.
It may be situated under the ground
or under the sea; it may be in distant
islands or coextensive with the world
of reality. It may be a house or a
palace that appears and disappears
with equal suddenness, or it may be
a little grass-covered hill that en-
compasses a whole vast and varie-
gated world with its peoples. It may
be reached through a cave, through
the waters of a lake, through a magic
mist – or simply through the granting
of sudden *insight*.

It is conceived as a land of peace and harmony, yet its inhabitants do not have to forego the principal diversion of heroic society, namely fighting. And what is more remarkable perhaps, their internal conflicts can be decided in favour of one side or the other by the intervention of a human being – a favourite motif in Irish, both in the early literature and in the modern folklore, and one which occurs also in the Welsh tale of *Pwyll*. In 'The Wasting Sickness of Cú Chulainn' the Ulster hero is asked to aid Labhraidh of the Swift Sword-hand against his enemies for the space of one day, in return for which he is promised the love of the beautiful Fann. In *Echtrae Laeghairi*, 'The Adventure of Laeghaire', a man emerges out of a mist before Crimhthann Cass, king of Connacht, and seeks his help in recovering his wife who has been abducted and whom he has failed to win back in battle. Laeghaire, Crimhthann's son, sets out with a force of fifty men in the wake of their supernatural visitant, and they duly overcome his enemies and recover his wife. Unlike Cú Chulainn, however, Laeghaire only returns to his father's kingdom to bid a last farewell; he and his men have taken wives from among the women of Magh Dá Cheo, 'The Plain of the Two Mists' (one of the evocative names given to the Irish otherworld), and they decide to remain there secure from the anxieties and infirmities of the mortal world.

And though it may seem strange that the happy folk of this 'Gentle Land' should pass some of their many idle hours in mutual slaughter, this is really only a minor manifestation of the general fluidity, or ambivalence, which characterises the Celtic otherworld. Being, as it is ultimately, an imaginative reflex of human attitudes and aspirations, this other kingdom assumes different forms according to the occasion and circumstance, but these forms are not sharply or consistently distinguished. When a mortal visits the otherworld by invitation, it is usually pictured as a land of contentment and joy. But when it is invaded by human heroes – a favourite theme in storytelling and one which is related to Cú Chulainn, Fionn and Arthur among others – then it wears a very different image. It may still be a country of riches and of wonders – and frequently the declared object of such heroic expeditions is to seize its treasures and its magical talismans – but inevitably its status relative to humanity has been transformed: its rulers and its welcoming hosts are now formidable and even monstrous enemies, fit to test the mettle of the greatest hero. In one of the tales Cú

Chulainn himself recounts an expedition of his to the Land of Shade. He found there a fortress surrounded by seven walls, and on each a palisade of irons on which were fixed nine heads. Hordes of serpents and other terrifying monsters were sent against him and his followers, but he slew them all, stormed the stronghold and carried off its treasures. In contexts of this nature the hero moves in a region of perilous adventure and of fearsome, malignant beings. The main emphasis is on the hazards he faces, on the dreadful ingenuity and magic which his supernatural foes have at their command and on all the awesome trappings – swordbridges, revolving castles, etc. – which characterise Irish and Welsh tales of the all but impregnable otherworld and which later become part of the routine paraphernalia of Arthurian romance.

The ambivalence of the otherworld emerges most clearly perhaps

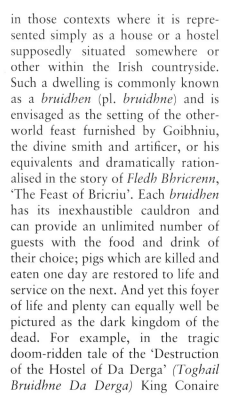

in those contexts where it is represented simply as a house or a hostel supposedly situated somewhere or other within the Irish countryside. Such a dwelling is commonly known as a *bruidhen* (pl. *bruidhne*) and is envisaged as the setting of the otherworld feast furnished by Goibhniu, the divine smith and artificer, or his equivalents and dramatically rationalised in the story of *Fledh Bhricrenn*, 'The Feast of Bricriu'. Each *bruidhen* has its inexhaustible cauldron and can provide an unlimited number of guests with the food and drink of their choice; pigs which are killed and eaten one day are restored to life and service on the next. And yet this foyer of life and plenty can equally well be pictured as the dark kingdom of the dead. For example, in the tragic doom-ridden tale of the 'Destruction of the Hostel of Da Derga' *(Toghail Bruidhne Da Derga)* King Conaire

Mór is drawn inexorably by way of a series of unwitting violations of his *geissi* or tabus towards the violent end that awaits him in the *bruidhen*. On his way there he has an ominous encounter with three horsemen accoutred all in red and riding red horses: 'the three "Reds" *(Deirg)* going to the house of "Red" *(Derg)*', in other words to the house of Da Derga, whose name means literally 'the god Derga'. Their mounts are 'the steeds of Donn Détscorach from the Otherworld', which merely confirms what is already evident from the context: that Derga is one and the same as Donn, god of the dead, and that those who, like Conaire, enter his abode are either dead or foredoomed.

The Feast of Samhain
But above all it is at the feast of Samhain, the first of November, that this

sombre image of the otherworld predominates. It may be remarked that the Celtic year was divided in two: a winter half beginning at Samhain, which may also have marked the commencement of the new year, and a summer half at Beltene or Cétshamhain, the first of May. These were further subdivided by the quarter-days of Imbolg, the first of February, and Lughnasadh, the first of August. Of these four festivals Samhain looms largest in the mythological record and its legends reveal certain features which find ready analogies in other traditions. In particular, it is well known that numerous peoples throughout the world have attached a very special significance to the juncture or interstice between two distinct temporal periods, regarding it in some sense as time outside of time or as a temporary resumption of mythic or primordial time. Similarly the Celts have treated the festival of Samhain – the duration of its celebration and more especially the eve of the feast-day – as a time apart which was charged with a peculiar preternatural energy, and within it they have concentrated many of their great mythic events. During this interval the normal order of the universe is suspended, the barriers between the natural and the supernatural are temporarily removed, the *sídh* lies open and all divine beings and the spirits of the dead move freely among human beings and interfere, sometimes violently, in their affairs. Conversely, this is the time when the *sídh* is most accessible and most vulnerable to those mortals daring enough to venture within its precinct. The hero of *Echtra Nerai*, 'The Adventure of Nera', is one of these.

On the eve of Samhain Ailill and Medhbh, king and queen of Connacht, offer the prize of his choice to whomsoever succeeds in putting a withe around the foot of either of two captives who had been hanged the previous day. Nera alone accepts the challenge. He goes to the gallows but he only succeeds in fixing the withe after the corpse has instructed him. The corpse then complains of thirst and Nera carries him on his back to a dwelling in which he finds water. Having replaced him on the gallows he returns to the royal court of Cruachain only to find it in flames and the severed heads of its people near by. As the attacking warriors move off Nera follows them into the Cave of Cruachain, a famous gateway to the otherworld. Once inside the *sídh* he is discovered but is permitted to remain. He takes a wife from among the women of the *sídh* and from her he learns that his vision of the destruction of the court of Cruachain was but a premonition: it will come true next Samhain, however, unless the *sídh* is ravaged before then. He sets out to bring warning to his own people, carrying with him fruits of summer — wild garlic and primrose and golden fern — to prove whence he had come, and he finds his friends still seated around the cauldron as he had left them, though much had befallen him in the meantime. When Samhain returns the Connacht warriors invade and plunder the *sídh* and carry off the three great treasures of Ireland. But Nera remains behind with his family in the *sídh* and there he will stay until Doomsday.

The legends of Samhain are legion. Muirchertach mac Erca and Crimhthann mac Fidhaigh perish through the sorcery of supernatural women, Cú Chulainn is visited by Lí Ban and Fann, and it is then that the great mythic battle of Magh Tuiredh is enacted. Constituting as it does a partial return to primordial chaos, Samhain is the appropriate setting for myths which symbolise the dissolution of established order as a prelude to its recreation in a new period of time. Famous kings and heroes die at Samhain — Muirchertach, Crimhthann, Diarmaid mac Cerbhaill, Conaire Mór, Cú Chulainn and others — sometimes within an elaborate scenario which is strongly redolent of ritual. It is a time of unbridled carousal, and the element of chaos and turbulence which is inherent in the feast emerges clearly in the story of *Mesca Ulad*, 'The Intoxication of the Ulstermen'. Faced with two invitations to go feasting, honour demands that the Ulstermen accept both. And so, having indulged themselves lavishly during the first half of the night at the court of Dún Dá Bhenn (in the present Co. Derry), they then set out for a second session at Cú Chulainn's fort of Dún Delga. They lose themselves en route and career headlong on a wild and drunken course throughout the length of Ireland, finally to arrive among their Munster enemies who first proceed to feast them and then all but succeed in roasting them alive in a burning house.

The Land of the Dead

So far it has been assumed here that the Celtic otherworld, Elysian or otherwise, and the realm of the dead are ultimately one. This is not necessarily inconsistent with the Irish tradition that the dead went to the kingdom of Donn: the otherworld is frequently conceived as a number of coexisting regions representing so many different aspects, and that the land of the dead should be especially differentiated as such is hardly surprising. The evidence for this view of the matter is too various to be resumed here, but it may be usefully exemplified from an Old Welsh poem entitled 'The Spoils of Annwn', *Preiddeu Annwn*, which tells — rather allusively it may be said — of a disastrous expedition to the otherworld, commonly known as Annwn, by Arthur and his men. Evidently the immediate object of the enterprise was to carry off the magic cauldron which is the characteristic appurtenance of the otherworld ruler in his role of dispenser of feasts, and it would appear from related texts that they succeeded in this — but only at great cost in lives, for of the three shiploads who embarked with Arthur only seven men returned.

The general structure of the poem suggests the common notion of the

otherworld as an island, but it is named by several different titles and described in terms which imply quite disparate conceptions of its character. In one stanza it appears as a kind of twilight underworld – as it does later in the Latin works of Walter Map and Giraldus Cambrensis – and once it is even referred to as *uffern*, 'Hell', showing early confusion with the Christian otherworld. In another stanza it becomes Caer Wydyr, 'Fortress of Glass', from whose sentinel Arthur and his company found it difficult to obtain response. This recalls an episode in Nennius's *Historia Brittonum* (of the early ninth century) which describes how the sons of Míl, having come to Ireland, took ship again to capture a tower of glass *(turris vitrea)* standing in the middle of the sea and were all of them drowned but for the crew of one ship which was unable to take part in the expedition. The occupants of the tower, when addressed, made no answer at all, maintaining the silence which is the distinguishing mark of the dead in Celtic as in certain other traditions. Quite clearly the glass tower (which incidentally Nennius quite wrongly associates with the sons of Míl) and the glass fortress are one and the same

Horse walking. Musée Municipal, Chalons-sur-Marne.

thing and both symbolise the realm of the dead.

Yet the Welsh poet did not think of Annwn solely, or primarily, as a silent land of the dead. One of the titles he gives it is Caer Feddwid, 'Court of Intoxication, or Carousal', and its staple drink is sparkling wine. It is also named Caer Siddi, and under this title it is described in a separate poem as a region in which sickness and old age are unknown, where there is enchanting music and a fountain flows with liquid sweeter than white wine – in other words it is 'The Land of the Living'. How then explain this apparent inconsistency? The answer is doubtless to be found in the early Irish Voyage tales which picture the otherworld as an archipelago of islands of varying and sometimes constrasting character which the intrepid mortal visits severally on his long Odyssey. For though the Welsh poem does not suggest that Arthur's exploit was another extended exploration of the supernatural, like Bran's or Mael Dúin's, nonetheless it is clearly a composite picture comprising just such a series of separate realisations of the otherworld as are found in these Irish Voyages. And the significant thing is that our poet, while obviously aware of their disparity, saw no inconsistency in conjoining the land of the dead and The Land of the Living as two aspects of the same otherworld.

It should perhaps be added that this underlying unity has not been universally accepted by modern scholars. It has sometimes been pointed out that those whom Irish (and indeed Welsh) literature records as visiting the otherworld are either heroes or kings, and the conclusion is drawn that the people at large must have shared a less distinguished afterlife – in the land of the dead. The flaw in this argument is its disregard for the fact that the early Celtic literatures are preponderantly aristocratic with an infinite capacity for ignoring the fortunes of the masses, whether in this life or in another. In fact, there is no good reason to suppose that the men and women of early Ireland thought very differently about these matters

from their descendants – further removed from them in time than in outlook – of whom the Elizabethan Father William Good remarked appositely: 'They suppose that the souls of such as are deceased go into the company of certain men, famous in those places, touching whom they retain still fables and songs.'

Opposite. Openwork bronze belt-hook from Hölzelsau, Austria, early fourth century B.C. It conforms to the basic imagery of a number of these La Tène belt-hooks: a small human figure flanked by beasts and birds, a composition which has been traced to the oriental motif of the 'Lord of Beasts' (see page 41). Prähistorische Staatssammlung, Munich.

Below. Statue from Boa Island in Lower Lough Erne, Co. Fermanagh. It shows two abbreviated human figures set back to back. Stylistically it invokes comparison with the so-called Maponus head from Corbridge, Northumberland (see page 32).

The Integral Tradition

After this brief survey of Celtic mythological remains it may occur to the reader to ask how much of their original significance these still retained when they were first written down by monastic scribes in the seventh century. But unfortunately, since we know so little about the actual content of the teaching imparted in the schools of the *filidh* and bards at that time or the nature of their commentaries on individual tales, the answer must be inferential and speculative. That some aura of their ancient efficacy still attached to the tales is beyond question, for they are not infrequently accompanied by a statement of special benefits that may be obtained by narrating them or by listening to them attentively: protection against sickness and death, prosperity, numerous progeny, and so on. And as has been pointed out, much the same virtues are ascribed to the traditional stories of India.

In some instances – kingship, royal inauguration, the notion of sovereignty, to take but a few related examples – there is abundant evidence that the symbolism and the function of both myth and ritual were still clearly perceived. It is also significant that so many pagan traditions and cults survived and flourished almost to our own day in consequence of the fact that they were accommodated under the capacious mantle of the Church and thereby acquired a rather spurious seal of respectability. Pagan deities were canonised out of number. Brighid became St Brighid and her cult continued uninterrupted. St Ann has attracted legends of the goddesses Anu and Áine. In several localities the memory remains of three holy sisters who cannot easily be dissociated from the trio of goddesses who figure so prominently in the early mythological legends . . . and so on.

This kind of assimilation is not peculiar to the insular Celtic countries, but apart from the fact that it is especially common there, it also reflects a more general tendency of the Christian Church to adapt itself as far as possible to indigenous customs and institutions, a tendency incidentally which had much to do with the remarkably peaceful transition from

Opposite above. Coin of the Osismii of Armorica, displaying certain features which are characteristic of the coinage of this area of Gaul. The obverse shows a head that is a striking blend of reality and abstraction. The hair, which is arranged in two rolls, is surmounted by a cross or four-pointed star, and the head is encircled by a beaded cord at the end of which another tiny head floats suspended. On the reverse side a horse with human head and an acrobatic rider 'en voltige' gallops above a prostrate human figure. All these several elements show a clear tendency to disintegrate into abstract forms and the rider has been virtually reduced to a rudimentary head. Most of the features of this and similar examples of Gaulish coinage are the result of stylistic evolution from imported prototypes, notably the stater of Philip II of Macedonia. Attempts have been made, however, to link some of these features to Gaulish myths and to the heroic traditions of the Ulster Cycle, but not with any conspicuous success. Bibliothèque Nationale, Paris.

Opposite below. The exterior of the Bronze Age tumulus of New Grange, Co. Meath, as it appeared before its restoration. Covering 1 acre (0.4 hectare), it is one of Europe's most impressive prehistoric monuments. The entrance, which is 60 feet (18 m) long, leads to the main chamber, which has a corbelled roof 19 feet (6m) high. The traditional name for New Grange, or for the complex of tombs to which it belongs, was *Bruigh na Bóinne* and it was regarded as the otherworld dwelling of the divine Oenghus Mac ind Óg.

paganism to Christianity. In part it was a matter of deliberate policy, as when the Christian metropolis of Ard Macha (Armagh) was sited within two miles of Emhain Mhacha, the capital of the Ulaidh, or when monastic foundations were established on the sites of druidic schools or pagan cult-centres – in fact there is a good deal of evidence to suggest that the Christian foundation at Ard Macha was established on or close by the site of an earlier pagan sanctuary. But even more perhaps did it reflect the natural reactions of a clergy who were the creatures of their environment and quite incapable of abandoning the traditions and the patterns of

thought which had moulded their own identities and which continued to inform the whole of contemporary society. The Irish Lives of the Saints offer a good illustration of this.

Beginning as reasonably sober documents, they gradually deteriorate into a 'literature of fantasy, which under the pretext of honouring the saints has so often obscured their memory'

and which so teems with mythological motifs that often the boundary between hagiography and mythology becomes largely notional.

In all the vast range of traditional material handled by the monastic scribes and *literati* nothing seems to have captured their imagination quite so completely as the theme of the voyage to the happy otherworld. Time after time they re-created this theme in lyric verse and imaginative prose, investing it with a magical attraction that has never palled. They were evidently intrigued by the changing image of the otherworld islands, its profusion of colour, its delicate interplay of contrasting conceptions of time and space, its sense of wonder and fantasy – properties which are not without analogies in the realm of Celtic art. Indeed Françoise Henry in her monumental study of Irish art has drawn a sensitive and revealing comparison between the accounts of the voyage to the otherworld and the complex, elusive ornament of Celtic art. She finds both characterised by the same aversion to rigidity and to barren realism and she sees in the illuminated pages of the Gospel books the artistic reflex of the polymorphic otherworld: 'This multiform and changing world where nothing is what it appears to be is but the plastic equivalent of that country of all wonders which haunts the mind of the Irish poets, and in which all those impossible fancies seem to come true

to which the world does not lend itself.'

Like the illuminated manuscript the otherworld tale offered an aesthetically appropriate medium for a combination of spiritual quest and vision which had existed before Christianity and which centuries later received, if not its finest, at least its most celebrated expression in the legends of the Grail. But, above all else, what ensured the otherworld tale its unique favour among the monastic poets and storytellers was its evident analogy with the biblical *terra repromissionis*, in Irish *Tír Tairngiri*, 'The Land of Promise'. In the earliest of the Voyage tales there is an implicit equation of the two which in several later tales gradually progresses towards an explicit identification as the overseas journey is transformed into a Christian *peregrinatio*, without however shedding any of its propensity to the marvellous. The culmination of this particular evolution was *Navigatio*

Above. Crudely carved god, horned and phallic, from Maryport, Cumbria. He carries a square shield and a heavy spear. Anne Ross identifies this and other similar British figures with the horned god as warrior. Netherhall Collection.

Opposite. One of two bronze heads mounted on a bronze-covered wooden bucket from a Celtic cemetery, probably of the first century A.D., at Aylesford, Kent. These elongated, almond-eyed faces have many analogues in earlier Celtic art; compare for example those on the Pfalzfeld pillar (see page 7). British Museum, London.

Brendani, 'The Voyage of St Brendan', which was written perhaps in the ninth century, was translated in due course into most of the languages of Europe and became Ireland's greatest single contribution to medieval European literature.

The Voyage tales directly affected by this Christian adaptation comprise only a relatively modest segment of the otherworld materials that have survived in Irish, not to speak of the whole range of mythological tradition that existed formerly. But nonetheless they do bring home the paradox that

the early mythographers from whom we have received the extant tradition had a transcendent and conflicting loyalty, since their spiritual purpose was to eradicate the religious system which gave the mythology its meaning; and clearly this casts a shadow of suspicion upon the integrity of their text. Insular mythology, we have often been reminded, is 'anarchical' and lacks the semblance of a system such as one finds in other Indo-European mythologies, in addition to which it is lamentably short on such items as cosmogony and eschatology.

And the conclusion is sometimes drawn that these are primary defects, on the assumption that they cannot be ascribed to the censorship of Christian monks 'who were . . . liberal enough to allow the preservation of episodes much stained with paganism, and features most shocking to the Christian mentality'. In point of fact, however, we can only surmise – perhaps quite erroneously – which details of pagan tradition were most likely to offend the moral sensibility of a seventh- or eighth-century monastic *literatus*. On the other hand, we

That some of these features had formerly been present is, in any case, not an unreasonable assumption. The cult of sacred trees which are evidently replicas of the Cosmic Tree and the various cosmographic traditions such as those relating to Tara argue strongly the existence of a cosmology and a cosmogony; the deluge and the plague which annihilated the peoples of Cesair and Partholón as likely as not continue native traditions of a cosmic cataclysm such as may be found in mythologies of beginnings throughout the world, and the manifold legends of the otherworld or land of the dead might very well conceal the debris of an eschatology. There are also many references and residual testimonies which indicate that there must once have been a vast body of ritual which fell into disuse at some stage and was noticed only casually in the written record. We know that in pre-Christian Celtic society such matters as these would have fallen within the purview of the druids (of whom Caesar says that they 'are concerned with the worship of the gods, look after public and private sacrifice, and expound religious matters'). At the same time Irish literature leaves us in little doubt that the druids were unremitting antagonists of the Church in a long-drawn-out ideological struggle which ended in the virtual annihilation of the druidic organisation. It is therefore not unreasonable to suppose that the monastic redactors did in fact suppress elements of druidic teaching and practice which they could not record without seeming to compromise the doctrines of the universal Church.

Obviously, then, what remains of Irish mythology – to name only the more richly documented of the two insular branches – is not the integral tradition, however archaic it may be in many respects, and one can only surmise how closely it approximates to that expounded by the druids in the fifth century when St Patrick first set foot in Ireland. Any assessment of the mythology which disregards this discrepancy, assuming the integrity of the written record, runs the risk of misrepresenting the character and scope of the mythology in its pre-Christian form. To say of the insular tradition, as one distinguished scholar has, that 'one searches in vain for traces of those vast conceptions of the origin and final destiny of the world which dominate other Indo-European mythologies', is a pardonable overstatement, but to conclude from this that such conceptions were foreign to the Celts is to presume too much.

One is reminded of an Old Irish text which tells of a visit by one of the otherworld people to St Columcille. After a preliminary conversation can be tolerably certain as to the kinds of myth that would inevitably have come into collision with the doctrines of his Church; and it goes without saying that they include those particular features in which Celtic religion and mythology are seen to be seriously deficient. There is therefore a strong presumption that these elements, in so far as they were present in the seventh century, were expunged by the monastic redactors because they found them blatantly irreconcilable with some of Christianity's principal tenets.

Columcille took his companion aside out of hearing of the monks who were with him 'in order to converse with him and to question him about the heavenly and earthly mysteries. While they were conversing from one hour to the same hour on the next day, Columcille's monks watched them from afar. When the conversation had come to an end, they suddenly beheld the young man vanishing from them. It is not known whither he went. When his monks begged Columcille to let them know something of the conversation, he said to them that he could not tell even one word of what had been told to him, and said that it was proper for men not to be told.' The matter of this little tale is quite apocryphal, but obviously not invented from nothing. The reticence which its author ascribes to Columcille was more probably a reflection of his own experience and outlook. And as for those 'heavenly and earthly mysteries' which were revealed to the saint, one wonders whether they may not indeed have had some bearing upon 'the origin and final destiny of the world'.

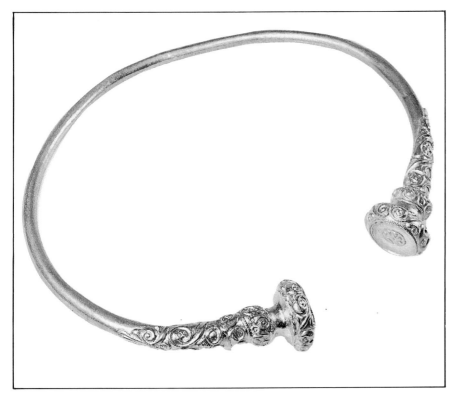

Top. Gold torc of the fourth century B.C. found with other objects in a chariot-burial at Waldalgesheim in the Rhineland. This find has given its name, Waldalgesheim, to a particular phase of La Tène artistic development. Rheinisches Landesmuseum, Bonn.

Above. The lid and handle of a bronze spouted flagon from a princess's grave (fourth century B.C.) at Reinheim near Saarbrücken. A horse-like animal with bearded human head stands upon the lid, while the upper handle shows a human head superimposed upon a ram-head. Landesmuseum für Vor- und Frühgeschichte, Saarbrücken.

Above. Bronze fair-lead, or harness-ring, with mask, third century B.C. Musée des Antiquités Nationales, St Germain-en-Laye.

Opposite. Detail of portal, Clonfert Cathedral, Co. Galway. The original church and monastery were founded here by St Brendan in 563, but the earliest part of the present church belongs to the twelfth century. The doorway with its elaborately decorated columns is surmounted by this gable comprising a columned arcade with human heads and above it a great triangle with rows of alternating marigolds and human heads. Some experts have seen these heads as a continuation of the familiar Celtic motif of *têtes coupées* or severed heads. Françoise Henry, however, holds that the Clonfert heads are romanesque features easily paralleled in churches of the period in western France. Nonetheless she notes that such heads set in niches are reminiscent of Gaulish monuments in the south of France, presumably Roqueperteuse and Entremont (see pages 100, 101 and 105), and that 'the likeness may not be fortuitous', which suggests that the heads on Irish churches of the romanesque period as well as their French counterparts may derive from Celtic prototypes.

Further Reading List

D'Arbois de Jubainville, H. *The Irish Mythological Cycle*, translated from the French by R. I. Best. Hodges and Figgis, Dublin, 1903

Cross. T. P., and Slover, C. H. *Ancient Irish Tales* (a collection of translations). Harrap, London, [1937].

Dillon, Myles. *Early Irish Literature*. The University of Chicago Press, Chicago, 1948.

Duval, Paul-Marie. *Les Dieux de la Gaule*. Payot, Paris, 1976.

Filip, Jan. *Celtic Civilization and its Heritage*. Publishing House of the Czechoslovak Academy of Sciences and ARTIA, Prague, 1960.

Gantz, Jeffrey. *Early Irish Myths and Sagas*. Penguin Books, Harmondsworth, London, 1981. *The Mabinogion*. Penguin Books, Harmondsworth, London, 1976.

Van Hamel, A. G. *Aspects of Celtic Mythology*. Rhys Lecture, British Academy, London, 1934.

Henry, Françoise. *Irish Art in the Early Christian Period to A.D. 800*. Methuen, London, 1965.

Jones, Gwyn and Thomas. *The Mabinogion* (translation of the Middle Welsh tales). Everyman's Library, Dent, London, 1950.

Le Roux, Françoise, and Guyonvarc'h, Christian-G. *Les Druides*. Ogam-Celticum, Rennes, 1978.

MacCulloch, John Arnott. *The Religion of the Ancient Celts*. Edinburgh, 1911. *Celtic Mythology*. Gray and Moore, Boston, 1918.

Meyer, Kuno, and Nutt, Alfred. *The Voyage of Bran*. Two volumes. David Nutt, 1895.

Murphy, Gerard. *Saga and Myth in Ancient Ireland*. Three Candles Press, Dublin, 1955. *Duanaire Finn, The Book of the Lays of Fionn*, Part III. The Educational Company of Ireland, Dublin, 1953.

O'Rahilly, Cecile (ed.). *Táin Bó Cuailnge from the Book of Leinster* (text and translation). Dublin Institute for Advanced Studies, 1967.

O'Rahilly, Thomas F. *Early Irish History and Mythology*. The Dublin Institute for Advanced Studies, Dublin, 1946.

Parry, Thomas. *A History of Welsh Literature*, translated from the Welsh by H. Idris Bell. Oxford, 1955.

Powell, T. G. E. *The Celts*. Thames and Hudson, London, 1958.

Rees, Alwyn and Brinley. *Celtic Heritage*. Thames and Hudson, London, 1961. Paperback edition 1973.

Rhys, John. *Lectures on the Origin and Growth of Religion as illustrated by Celtic Heathendom* (The Hibbert Lectures, 1886). Third edition. Williams and Norgate, London, 1898. *Celtic Folklore, Welsh and Manx*, Oxford, 1901.

Ross, Anne. *Pagan Celtic Britain*. Routledge and Kegan Paul, London, 1967. Paperback edition Cardinal, London, 1974.

Sjoestedt, Marie-Louise. *Gods and Heroes of the Celts*, translated from the French by Myles Dillon. Methuen, London, 1949.

Vendryes, Joseph. *La religion des Celtes*, in 'Mana, Introduction à l'Histoire des Religions', 2, III. Presses Universitaires de France, Paris, 1948.

de Vries, Jan. *Keltische Religion*. W. Kohlhammer Verlag, Stuttgart, 1961.

Acknowledgments

Photographs. Archaeological Survey of India, New Delhi 41 bottom left; Archives Photographiques, Paris 40; Ashmolean Museum, Oxford 80, 105 top; L. Aufsberg, Sonthofen 35; Belzeaux – Zodiaque 8, 11 top, 50, 60, 61, 65, 85, 87, 102, 108 top, 110, 116, 117, 139 right; Bibliothèque Nationale, Paris 133 top; British Museum, London frontispiece 45, 59 top, 59 bottom, 79, 80-1, 112; City Museum and Art Gallery, Gloucester 32 right; Commission of Public Works in Ireland, Dublin, 43, 56 left, 61, 90, 91 top right, 107, 111 top, 127 left, 133 bottom; Corinium Museum, Cirencester 91 bottom right; Dieuzaide – Zodiaque 68, 69, 71; C. M. Dixon, Dover 11 bottom, 138; Franceschi – Zodiaque 46 top right, 47, 53, 88-9, 100; Photographie Giraudon, Paris 26, 28-9, 29 left, 33 left; Simone Guiley-Lagache, Paris 99; Hamlyn Group Picture Library 67, 82-3, 103; Irish Tourist Board, Dublin 58, 66, 106 top, 111 bottom left, 111 bottom right, 123 bottom, 131; Landesbildstelle Württemberg 124; Mansell Collection, London 96; Merseyside County Museum, Liverpool 115; Malcolm Murray, Edinburgh 127 right; Musée Archéologique, Dijon 9 left, 9 centre, 9 right, 12, 13 left, 13 centre, 13 right; Musée Borély, Marseilles half-title page, 19; Musée des Antiquités Nationales, Saint-Germain-en-Laye 21, 29 right, 46 top left, 91 left; Musée Historique, Orleans 15; Museum of Antiquities of the University and the Society of Antiquaries, Newcastle-upon-Tyne 30, 32 left, 36, 41 bottom right, 70-1, 73, 76 right, 84, 98; Nationalmuseet, Copenhagen 39, 42-3, 55 top, 120-1, 123 top; National Museum of Ireland, Dublin 11 top, 14, 17, 74, 92-3, 97, 104, 104-5, 109, 114, 118, 137; National Museum of Wales, Cardiff 57; Photoresources, Dover 30-1, 55 bottom, 63, 75, 78, 95 left, 95 right, 106 bottom, 119, 130, 134, 135; Rheinisches Landesmuseum, Bonn 37, 81, 139 top left; Rheinisches Landesmuseum, Trier 33 right; Jean Roubier, Paris 22, 27, 34, 38 left, 38 right, 41 top, 44 bottom, 46 bottom, 48, 51, 52, 77, 101, 105 bottom, 108 bottom, 113, 128-9, J. K. St Joseph, Cambridge 120; Scala, Antella 23; Seminario & Centro Camuno di Studi Preistorici, Brescia 49; Staatliche Konservatoramt, Saarbrücken 76 left, 139 bottom left; Dr H. Taylor, Cambridge 126; Ulster Museum, Belfast 10; Württembergisches Landesmuseum, Stuttgart 24, 56 right, 62, 125, 136; Zodiaque, Saint-Léger-Vauban 18, 18-19, 70; Zodiaque – Rheinischeslandesmuseum, Bonn 7.

Index